LOSING BALANCE

THE DE-DEMOCRATIZATION OF AMERICA

Other Books by William P. Kreml

The Anti-Authoritarian Personality

The Middle Class Burden

Relativism and the Natural Left

A Model of Politics

Psychology, Relativism and Politics

LOSING BALANCE

THE DE-DEMOCRATIZATION OF AMERICA

WILLIAM P. KREML

M.E. Sharpe, Inc.
Armonk, New York
London, England

Library of Congress Cataloging-in-Publication Data

Kreml, William P.
    Losing balance: the de-democratization of America / by William P. Kreml
      p. cm.
    Includes bibliographical references and index.
    ISBN 0-87332-846-9 (cloth)
    1. Political participation—United States. 2. Politics, Practical—United States.
    3. Lobbying—United States. 4. Pressure groups—United States. 5. United States—
    Politics and government—1945–   I. Title.
    JK1764.K73   1991
    324′.0973—dc20   91-9148
                                                 CIP

Printed in the United States of America

MV 10 9 8 7 6 5 4 3 2 1

To
America's Next Generation

Contents

Foreword   ix

Acknowledgments   xi

Introduction   xiii

1 • Jefferson and the Generations   3

2 • Private and Public Domains   15

3 • The Washington Beltway   29

4 • The Lawyer-Lobbyist   43

5 • The Elections Industry   53

6 • The Levels of Government   65

7 • America's Political Parties   75

8 • Congress   89

9 • The Chief Executive   103

10 • A New World   115

11 • The National Press   123

12 • The Academy   131

13 • Remedies   139

14 • Jefferson's and Lincoln's Lessons   153

Index   161

Foreword

In 1980, William Kreml, a political scientist at the University of South Carolina, entered the Democratic senatorial primary against Senator Ernest F. Hollings with an unusual purpose. He argued, in a campaign that received national attention, that the American political system was no longer capable of dealing effectively and fairly with the increasingly complex issues of the late twentieth century. Further, he predicted that the government would soon sustain massive budget deficits. Most significantly, he argued that the root cause of these governmental failures was structural. The government, he said, had altered its institutions in a way that no longer permitted it to govern either effectively or fairly.

In 1984, Professor Kreml entered selected Democratic presidential primaries and again alerted the public to the structural causes of America's governmental difficulties. Then Kreml returned to his writing. Here, in *Losing Balance: The De-Democratization of America*, he describes America's political failings in the context of the imbalances of four fundamental preconstitutional tensions. What Kreml claims, quite credibly I think, is that each of these tensions—the private-to-public tension, the legal-to-political tension, the majoritarian-to-antimajoritarian tension, and the centrifugal-to-centripetal tension—has been distorted in a way that has seriously impaired America's unwritten constitution.

Specifically, in the Beltway chapter but also in the chapters on

Washington's lawyer-lobbyists and the elections industry, Kreml reviews how Washington's allegedly private, ancillary institutions have distorted and weakened America's governing institutions. In the chapters on the governmental institutions themselves, he properly cites their failing structural integrity as a leading cause of the country's recent governmental failures. In a year in which the government's forecast deficit was pegged at 60 billion dollars and at this writing has ballooned by a factor of six, Kreml's analysis becomes poignant indeed.

What Kreml contends is that no government can govern either effective or fairly if it does not maintain reasonable balance across the often conflicting pushes and pulls of its underlying organizing principles. In order to maintain the proper prudential balance, Kreml argues, political systems must sustain a vigorous public dialogue that includes discussion of *how* government decisions get made. As Kreml points out, the manner in which America arrives at its political decisions has changed dramatically for the worse in recent years and the democratic nature of the American polity has suffered in the process. *Losing Balance* defines those changes within an original and conceptually rich context. It also makes recommendations for how the nation can stem the de-democratizing process that has afflicted it over the last twenty years.

This is a book that seriously addresses fundamental questions of importance to all "small d" democrats. A thoughtful national dialogue based on the questions Kreml poses would improve the quality of public discussion considerably. And redressing the imbalances he identifies in the structure of American government would raise the level of democracy and increase the effectiveness and fairness of public policy to an even greater extent.

—Robert D. McClure, Professor of Political Science
and Public Affairs and Associate Dean
The Maxwell School of Citizenship and Public Affairs
Syracuse University

Acknowledgments

My deep thanks to Peter Sederberg, Daniel Postel, and Nancy Posselt for their helpful suggestions with this manuscript. I also wish to thank the Department of Government and International Studies of the University of South Carolina, its chair William Mishler, and the secretarial staff, for their assistance in preparing the work for publication. Any errors are my responsibility alone.

Introduction

As the Framers sought to provide for a more perfect union in the 1787 Philadelphia Convention, they wrote a Constitution that in its brevity and flexibility encouraged a process of ongoing perfection. Over the past 200 years, the American Constitution has changed markedly, most visibly through the adoption of twenty-six amendments. Less visibly, but no less significantly, changes have taken place in the constitutional order that are best reflected in the evolution of the usages, customs, and traditions of the American political system.

As a result of those changes, America's unwritten constitution is a very different set of political instructions today than it was 200 years ago. The notion of an unwritten constitution is hardly new, but analyses of American democracy have focused far less frequently on it than they have on the written Constitution. *Losing Balance: The De-democratization of America* is an examination of the current state of the unwritten American Constitution. It specifically scrutinizes those changes in America's institutions that have occurred in recent years and the loss of democracy that has attended those changes. I consider de-democratization to be nothing less than a falling away from the golden mean of democracy that exist between the two modern perversions of democracy: dictatorship on the one hand, and the excessive influence of today's aristocracy of interests on the other. The slide into de-

democratization can happen rapidly, as it did with the Weimar Republic in 1932–33, or it can occur gradually, as with the fall of republican Rome or of Periclean Athens. But no matter how rapid the decline, history surely teaches that democracy is a fragile thing and that it must continually be renewed in order to continue to exist.

Throughout history, de-democratization has invariably meant at least two things for the polities that it affected. First, it has always meant the end of that equitable participation of the people, both as individuals and as a whole, that in turn ensured the equity of public policy. Second, it has always foretold a reduction of that energy and vitality that come through the contributions of a robust political opposition and that ensure the healthy renewal of the society.

This set of essays on the American process of de-democratization grows out of two visions. The first is a speculation, really, upon what antifederalists such as Richard Henry Lee, George Mason, Patrick Henry, and Elbridge Gerry would say about the American government were they here today. The second focuses on how the informal, preconstitutional balances implicit in the original Constitution and the Bill of Rights have recently been disturbed beyond anything that the antifederalists, and even the federalists, could have imagined. Put another way, the focus here is on what some call America's "living Constitution" or on those alterations in the day-to-day workings of the American government that have affected it in profound and far-reaching ways.

The following essays, in short, define America's current governmental crisis as largely extraconstitutional in nature. Further, they place much of the responsibility for the current crisis of our government on the present generation of officeholders as well as on those who have assisted these officeholders in their growing isolation from the American people. *Losing Balance: The De-democratization of America* calls for a new understanding of the balances between private and public realms, legal and political jurisdictions, singular and majoritarian interests, and, most importantly, the structurally centrifugal and centripetal governmental arrangements that must exist in any democratic political arrangement. It calls, ultimately, for a reconstituting of America's political structures in light of the recent changes in the American constitutional order.

1

Jefferson and the Generations

The Current Decline

Thomas Jefferson charged each generation with ensuring that America's constitutional order remain equal to the task of public governance. Arguing that "laws and institutions must go hand in hand with progress of the human mind," Jefferson contended that "as manners and opinions change with the change of circumstances, institutions must advance also and keep pace with the times."[1] Above all, Jefferson knew that each generation would pay a cumulative price for a preceding generation's derelictions. He knew that constitutional revitalization is an ongoing matter and that when the prospects of a generation fail to approach those of the one preceding it, we should suspect that the nation's institutions have not kept pace with the times.

Over the last quarter century, the decline in America's economic and political standing, its foreign and domestic debts, its trade imbalances, its abnormally high interest rates, its recurring inflation, and the declining prospects of a goodly number of its citizens have become clear to all. Perhaps less apparently, these indicators have declined even more dramatically when they are compared with those of a number of nations in Europe and even Asia, against whom we should measure ourselves. As a result of the decline, the ability of many Americans in the next generation to purchase a home, to receive a reasonable education, or even to live as comfortably as their parents did is in jeopardy. This situation has arisen, in some part, because of specific public policy failures. But even more, it has arisen because of the failure of the current generation to revitalize the constitutional order in a way that Jefferson, were he alive today, would have required. In more concrete terms, many of the nation's fundamental ills can be laid at the doorstep of the current generation of officeholders. It is they who have encouraged changes in the government in order to pursue their own political careers and to protect a coterie of private, largely economic interests to whom they are increasingly beholden.

Precisely what the current generation of officeholders, in league with private political interests and a top-heavy collection of political accessories who have inflicted themselves on the American government, has done to place the next generation in jeopardy is something that the new generation has every right to know—and every right to reverse. As the next generation will soon assume responsibility for the public affairs of this country, it will, in its turn, also become the trustee for the generation that follows it.

Most criticisms that are made of the American government today are substantive, focusing on the seemingly irresolvable difficulties of the federal deficit, the trade deficit, the sale of American assets to foreign interests, and the like. But these difficulties have not come upon us without profound causes. These causes are identifiable and they are, as we should have expected, as political as they are economic in their nature. The next generation's ability to reverse America's decline depends on its ability to understand what the current generation has done, not merely to our economic institutions but, more importantly, to the American political arrangement as well.

The Preconstitutional Order

In creating the formal and informal arrangements of America's union, the Framers at the Philadelphia Convention and the anti-federalists who originally opposed the Constitution did several things. Patently, they agreed on a structure of government that provided for the most dispersed configuration of legislative, executive, and judicial powers that the world had ever known. Constrained within a dispersed structure, most of the delegates argued, government would be less likely to overreach its boundaries and invade the liberties that they held dear. In concert with the antifederalists who eventually gave their consent to the Constitution, they agreed, in effect, that certain preconstitutional balances would keep the American governmental order from being either wholly ineffective on the one hand or overbearing with regard to the American citizenry on the other.

Underlying and informing the formal separation of powers, for instance, less obvious understandings were significant. Perhaps the most important was the delegates' and the antifederalists' conception of the separate and balanced public and private domains. Borrowing from the English experience, they took care to protect a sphere of private life within which American citizens would enjoy at least the same propertied and contractual freedoms that the English yeoman had long enjoyed. The federalists wanted no smaller arena of private activity for America's citizens than the mother country had provided. The antifederalists, though they too viewed the private domain favorably, felt that the cap-

ture of the government by large commercial and financial interests necessitated a Bill of Rights that would protect the public as
well as the private rights of citizens.

Another of the delegates' preconstitutional assumptions concerned the division of legal and political jurisdictions. By the
close of the seventeenth century, the tradition of the English
common law was viewed as a central protection against public
invasion of the private domain. In the American constitutional
arrangement, the common law similarly was allowed a broad
jurisdictional arena. Here the antifederalists disagreed, drawing
upon the early-seventeenth-century sense of the common law as
a protector of the collected citizenry against Stuart-like excesses
that might come from an undemocratic government.

Another unspoken preconstitutional assumption underpinned
the 1787 Constitution. The delegates were mindful of the necessity for all public institutions to balance the claims of individuals
seeking protection from the government against the essentially
majoritarian claims of those aggregated citizens who wanted the
government to do something for them. The Framers—and I mean
the federalists and the antifederalists combined—felt, in other
words, that the particular or individualistic forces of the society
must balance the claims of the larger citizenry for governmental
action. Fearing the majority, the federalists preferred a government that would respond to the singular rather than the aggregate
claim. The antifederalists disagreed here too, but, again, the Bill
of Rights assuaged their fear by assuring protection for those
majoritarian political activities that they expected would be essential for the representation of their interests.

Finally, in their attempt to stabilize the preconstitutional order,
the federalists and the antifederalists drew upon one other balance. The federalists in the convention felt that the new government should favor the centrifugal, or decentralizing, forces of a
governmental structure over what they considered to be the inevi-

table tendency of all governments to centralize their institutions and abuse power. Though the antifederalists properly saw the new Constitution's centrifugal arrangements as checking the public aggregations that would lead to popular government, they believed sufficiently in the centripetal nature of the Bill of Rights that they confidently expected aggregate political activity to balance the centrifugal structure of the Constitution's original seven articles. These four balances, then—the private-to-public, the legal-to-political, the antimajoritarian-to-majoritarian, and the centrifugal-to-centripetal structural—constitute the essential preconstitutional balances of the American government.

In designing this government, particularly with regard to the balance of its centrifugal and centripetal structures, the federalists and the antifederalists felt that, overall, they had worked out a reasonable mix of institutions for the American constitutional order. As time has passed, however, these institutions have been altered as a result of the self-serving adaptations of the order that the government's officeholders and their supporting interests have brought about.

As a result of these adaptations or, better, maladaptations, that will be discussed throughout, and as a result of more recent changes in the American private domain that will be discussed in the next chapter, events have occurred that have particularly disturbed America's usually easy confidence in its ability to deal with its political problems. The first is that the world, as well as America's relationship to it, has changed markedly. For a goodly time, our country, bordered by two large oceans and two small nations, prospered both economically and politically from its isolation from a very distant world. Now our nation is more a part—and an increasingly smaller part—of a less forgiving world. America's share of world economic production has fallen from 50 percent in the late 1940s to below 20 percent today. More important, annual increases in American productivity that had averaged 3 percent from 1946 to 1968 fell to 2 percent from 1968 to 1973, fell further to 1 percent from 1973 to 1978, and have progressed only marginally in the years since. As a result, any improvement in the standard of living of most middle-class families has come almost exclusively through the innovation of the double-wage household. At that, many have fallen out of the middle class, which had been America's greatest protector of its political stability and equity.

But something even more profound than the passing of America's economic domination of the world has occurred in recent years. Under the pressure of those who would not postpone what they believed to be entitled increases in their own standards of living, and with the complicity of those officeholders who have weakened the structural integrity of the government in order to fulfill these expectations and their own expectations of incumbency, the government's ability to understand the public interest and create productive and equitable public policies has been diminished. The informal processes of American government—that set of daily routines, understandings, and all-too-comfortable "networking" that currently typifies it—have altered what is usually called America's unwritten constitution so that the government of today is a far different thing from what it was even a short time ago. The result is that America's preconstitutional balances have been altered significantly in recent years.

Perhaps the debilitating and inequitable structural changes that America's current generation of officeholders with their private interests have inflicted on the nation are best understood as creating three pernicious political developments: (1) an increased isolation of each officeholder from the general public so that he or she is farther from the public trust than at any time in the history of the Republic; (2) an increased isolation of each officeholder from his or her fellow officeholders and from the political parties to which each pretends allegiance; and (3) an increased isolation of each officeholder from the public, ostensibly democratic institutions within which each ostensibly serves. What has resulted from these developments has been an increasingly self-contained political linkage of each officeholder to local, private interests, who in return for their electoral support expect the officeholder to protect those interests to the exclusion of the general good.

Private interests and political incumbency have always reinforced each other to a degree, in the American political system and elsewhere. But the recent significant changes in the American government's unwritten constitution evidence a marked increase in the unwillingness on the part of the nation's officeholders to consider the general welfare as more important than the welfare of their separate constituencies. Though these changes have been made through alterations in America's unwritten, not written, constitution, they are no less damaging to the general welfare. Because they have resulted from fundamental changes in the method of electing public officeholders and in the internal procedures of the government's principal institutions, these developments now ensure that only the least challenging of America's public difficulties, and the least controversial of possible solutions for these difficulties, will survive political debate. Obviously, this situation benefits the current generation of officeholders. With the government unable to adopt innovative but necessary policies for the good of the entire nation, each officeholder has more than ever assured himself or herself that what might prove embarrassing to them in a quest for reelection is kept from public consideration.

Perhaps predictably, today's officeholder argues that the changes detailed above mark a progression to a modern governmental form. This simply is not so. The active involvement of officeholders in the changes that have taken place within the government has stifled the government and made it less democratic. At a superficial level, the government has been forced into a condition of gridlock. At a more fundamental level, that broad participation of America's citizenry in the government that the antifederalists were particularly concerned with in their Bill of Rights has been endangered. America is less of a democracy today for that loss of citizen participation.

Why are these recent alterations in the constitutional order so costly to the nation? As the next generation of American citizens must understand better than does the current one, the economic and political difficulties that America faces today are not solely those of the budget deficit, the trade deficit, the selling of American assets overseas, and the like. The real political difficulties that have been brought about by America's governmental changes are both more immediate and more profound. The United States today lags behind many other industrial nations in health care (20 percent of Americans have no health insurance), in infant mortality (America now ranks seventeenth among the industrial nations), and, most damagingly, in education (cross-national studies consistently place America's students below those of other industrial nations, particularly in the sciences and mathematics). Drugs and crime afflict our nation's inner cities to such a degree that the principal cause of death among young black males is now homicide. These political realities are in great part the progeny of America's recent governmental alterations. For the first time in the history of our nation, Americans must now consider whether the United States government may no longer be the government that most of them have led themselves to believe it is. It may no longer be the best government in the world.

The Next Generation's Challenge

In retrospect, the coming of the United States into the world political community as a nation far different from any that had preceded it marked more than a change in the fortunes of a single people. The creation of the government of the United States marked a historic moment for all political history. The impact of this moment was noted by, among others, the Constitution's principal drafter, James Madison, who felt that the greatest threat to American democracy would not come from the kings, aristocracies, or established churches of the Old World. The threat would come, Madison thought, from the potential excesses of democracy.

In *The Federalist*, No. 10, and elsewhere, Madison contended that an overly democratic political system might fall prey to the democratic pressures of its general citizenry. Those pressures, Madison feared, would alter the foundational balances of the limited democracy that the American government provided in favor of too much democracy. To prevent such an alteration, Madison's design for the American Republic forbade such democratic guarantees as pure popular representation and included constitutional safeguards that he hoped would prevent the political overwhelming of the government by unpropertied citizens. In the United States, as in so many other nations of the world, even the limited promise of democratic government was compromised from the beginning.

But if Madison's fears centered around the potential for democratic excess on the part of unpropertied citizens, our government's current difficulties have not originated from an imbalance of governmental access on the part of the greater, unpropertied population. Our government's difficulties have resulted from those distortions of the governmental structure that stem from the ever easier access to the government that is enjoyed by America's private economic institutions. That access has diminished the ability of the government to address the public's needs. Though, again, such a diminishing of the government's ability to govern was no more among the corruptions of the Constitution that Madison or the antifederalists feared than was the role of the propertied citizens in that diminishing, that is precisely what has occurred. And it has occurred without violating a word of the constitutional document itself.

As the United States enters its third constitutional century, a rebalancing of the American preconstitutional and constitutional orders is both necessary and proper. That rebalancing may require minor revisions of the written Constitution; our dispersed constitutional structure may need some formal, centripetally directed updating. More certainly, however, that rebalancing will require revisions in the informal structuring of the government's processes. Surely, it will also require a reaffirmation in a modern context of what was explicit in the arguments of the antifederalists, as well as what was implicit in their acceptance of the Constitution in return for the federalists' acceptance of the Bill of Rights. The next generation must restore the four preconstitutional balances that the American constitutional order always assumed.

In sum, as the next generation stands to be injured by the recent alterations in the unwritten constitution, it will need to develop standards for the third century of American democracy that redresses those alterations. If the genius of the Constitution's Framers, combined with the genius of the antifederalist advocates of the Bill of Rights, was evidenced by their combined ability to find proper balances within and without the structures and the processes of their newly created government, it will depend upon the genius of the next generation to reset those balances.

Let us not forget that the federalists and the antifederalists purposely placed a vitalizing flexibility into the American Constitution. But they did so in order to enable our government to respond to the exigencies of a changing world, not in order to have the custodians of that Constitution bend its structure to their own and to their narrowest constituencies' purposes. Demands on America's national government have clearly grown over the past two centuries. It is a truism to say now that coordination within and between the separated centers of America's political arrangement is more essential today than it ever has been before. But the members of the current generation of officeholders, again largely for their own convenience and without regard to the larger necessities of the American people as a whole, have ignored their responsibility to engage in such coordination, much less to engage in constitutional revitalization. They have, again, adjusted the processes of our government, as well as the preconstitutional and constitutional balances of our larger political system, in the opposite direction.

Jefferson's admonition that each generation must undertake its own revision of the Constitution in order to provide for its own needs and the needs of the nation is therefore doubly apt today. The United States, and its government, is fully one generation behind where they both should be. If this nation and its people are to recoup their fortunes, they must follow Jefferson's prescription for the revitalization of the constitutional order. They must rebalance the current generation's economic and political selfishness with a greater concern for America's general welfare than any generation has yet shown.

Note

1. Donald L. Robinson, ed., *Reforming American Government*. Boulder, CO: Westview Press, 1985, p. xi.

2

Private and Public Domains

The Reciprocal Relationship

America's federal government is more important to the American
people today than it has ever been. In part, it is more important
because of the faltering position of the United States in the
world. But in greater part, it is more important because
America's political arrangements reflect an increasing distur-
bance in the most important of its preconstitutional balances—
that between the private and public domains.

America's private domain, like its global position, is unique.
Nowhere in the world are the fundamental economic decisions
concerning productivity and distribution so firmly in the hands of
private institutions. Throughout virtually all of American history,
the nation's political culture, as well as its formal political arrangements, relegated the government to a subordinate economic
position in the belief that America's private institutions would
produce abundant wealth and distribute that wealth appropriately.
Today, those institutions perform both tasks less ably than ever
before. And although American political culture, built around the

English common law of property, contract, and tort, continues to fortify Americans' confidence in the private economy, that confidence is no longer balanced by a similar view of the public domain. This imbalance of confidence, too, exacts a stern price from our country's economic and political well-being.

Changes in the Private-Public Relationship

Two significant legal changes in the relationship between individuals and economic institutions have accounted for the enlargement of the private domain's role in the American economy. The first has been the radically reduced influence of what are now only nominal owners of private economic institutions. Corporation owners today are mere investors, divested from responsibility for the decisions of independent managers. The long evolution of business organizations away from what were originally only joint stock companies has ended in nearly complete administrative autonomy for corporate management. The autonomy of this management constituency in the context of the American political system has had a significant impact on the balance between America's private and public domains.

The second and more significant legal change in the relationship between individuals and economic institutions involves the responsibility of private managers to the community at large. Reversing centuries of common law–developed private responsibility, current law allows a private institution's management to protect itself behind a corporate veil. These legal changes have both insulated private management from the public and enhanced the power of the private domain relative to that of the public.

Two nonlegal changes within the private corporation have also had a direct impact upon the economic well-being of the nation. Each involves a manner of doing business that in the short term facilitates what may be in the best interest of the corporation but in the long term contributes to a deterioration in the health of American corporations and the American economy generally.

The first such change has been in the structure of the corporation: specifically, the placement of an excessive number of personnel into private management hierarchies. All institutions, private and public, tend to expand their membership to the degree that the external environment permits. Subcomponents of any institution, similarly, will expand their jurisdictions to the degree that the environment of the larger institution permits. Because of the dominant position of American business vis-à-vis the remainder of the world following World War II, America's private economic institutions multiplied their layers of management over and over again. Further, as prices for goods and services within what were increasingly oligopolistic arenas of industry and finance became administered rather than competitive, the expansion of management hierarchies was permitted to grow all the more. Incentives for corporations to do basic industrial research, develop new products, produce new wealth, and generally remain efficient in their production of wealth grew increasingly independent of market considerations.

The second nonlegal change that has adversely affected America's economic well-being has to do with the political legitimacy of America's economic institutions. Ostensibly, the more private a nation's productive arrangements, the more individualistic and competitive must be the ethic that supports them. But in fact, if the reality of a market obeys a competitive ethic, fewer, not more, management personnel will attain their desired level of achievement within private institutions. And, if a significant number of private-management employees fail to obtain a desired level of compensation and stature, the political legitimacy of a largely private system of economic productivity will diminish accordingly. To ensure political support for what some would have us believe is still a competitive economic system, more competitors must succeed than would do so in a truly competitive economic situation. The resulting compensatory rewards to those who are in actuality producing less wealth than they are being rewarded for invariably weakens the economic system.

Largely as a result of these changes in the private domain, the American productive system today is no longer as competitive as it was even a few years ago. Even with a spate of recent trimmings, excessive numbers of well-compensated upper-to-middle-management employees in basic manufacturing industries, as well as in the service industries of insurance, real estate, banking, and investment, are being retained by America's corporations. The important political expectation among America's middle class that it will be ensured of employment at a reasonable level of reward is still fulfilled. America's universities and colleges, as portals to middle-class positioning, contribute to and benefit from this expectation as well.

The gap between middle-class reward expectations and the productivity of private economic institutions is more costly for America today than ever before. But as the political legitimacy of the productive system is still unquestioningly endorsed by the politically powerful white-collar staffs, it remains difficult for the public domain to impose standards of economic productivity on the private domain. Insistence on the employment of private workers in excess of the number that would minimally be required to achieve maximum productivity does not only contribute to a lack of economic productivity within the American economy. It also contributes to a corresponding dearth and underpayment of teachers, health workers, environmental workers, and those who labor in a variety of other necessary but public occupations.

As a further consequence of this imbalance between private and public domains, America's private institutions have recently been permitted to borrow almost at will from the natural riches of the country. They have done so ostensibly to enhance the wealth of the nation as well as the profitability of their own enterprises. But these private productive institutions have not increased their productivity through such easy access to the nation's natural wealth. And despite some improvement on the part of some more responsible corporations and the recent passage of the first meaningful environmental protection law in the last sixteen years, the private domain still has not accepted its obligation to repay the public domain for its contributions to polluted air, impure water, deforestation of the land, and the like. To restore the private-public balances of this country, the public domain must require that private institutions begin to make a fair contribution to the restoration of all aspects of America's common wealth.

To the degree that private institutions insist upon considering only their own well-being, the public domain is now entitled to require that those institutions help balance the national ledger with higher productivity, heightened environmental protection, and higher contributions to the restoration of human capital. Because short-term economic gain has proven to restrict initiatives toward long-term economic productivity, environmental well-being, and, perhaps most importantly, contributions to human capital, the government must be capable of ensuring that the larger private-to-public balance in America is restored. But the recent de-democratization of the government, in response to the selfish requirements of the current generation of public office-holders and private-domain personnel, makes that task all the more difficult.

The Productive Imperative

The idea of a necessary reciprocity between America's private and public domains is straightforward but not always simple, for there is room for reasonable political disagreement over the boundaries of these jurisdictions. The compelling need for reciprocity, however, requires a government that more carefully than ever guards the public interest. Also requiring political consideration are those imbalances in the private-to-public reciprocity that go beyond the relationships of individuals to modern private enterprises; the hollowing out of the educational, health, and safety functions of the public domain; or the public cost of the private domain's usage of public resources. Although founded as a nation wherein post roads, canals, harbors, and ports were at least in part a public responsibility, and although enjoying throughout its short history periods of active public involvement in ensuring the public's well-being, the United States now places more responsibility for the wealth of the nation on private managers than at any time since the late nineteenth century. Requiring an accounting for that responsibility has always been legitimate for the public domain and it is even more legitimate now.

Throughout nearly all of the two hundred years of this Republic, the American citizenry took it on faith that their private institutions were both as inherently productive and as responsive to their public obligations as they should have been. To be sure, it is more difficult for a government to involve itself in private investment and productivity today than it was for the government to build post roads, dig canals, and subsidize shipbuilding, and the like 200 years ago. But the recent decline in the competitiveness of the American economy, along with the recent alteration of the distributive results of the American economy in favor of those in control of the private domain, speaks to the need for the government to do more with regard to productivity than it has done in recent years. Whether by limiting speculative but unproductive investment strategies that do not add to the common wealth or by restricting the private domain's nearly exclusive role in providing distributional allocations among the citizenry, the public domain needs to balance the private domain far better than it does at present. The insulation of modern America's corporate management, along with the recent rise of a seemingly permanent underclass of unemployed and underemployed Americans, signals the need for a rebalancing of America's private-to-public domains.

To enhance the nation's productivity and to address the current maldistribution of the nation's allocations, the American government must now take several specific steps. These steps include such relatively simple measures as the enactment of revisions in the tax laws that include disincentives for consumption and incentives for saving and investment. These are obvious starting points toward increased productivity. A return to a truly progressive income tax and a meaningful array of excise taxes is also necessary. But more than a revised taxation format, a discouragement of consumption, and an adjustment of the tax burden will be required.

The principal reason why the public domain has not addressed the private domain's abandonment of productive and distributive responsibilities is that the government has restructured itself, largely abandoning the antifederalist-inspired guarantees of majoritarian democratic government in the original political order. It has put in their place a more highly centrifugal structure than even the Framers preferred.

Put simply, the American government has fragmented itself to the point that it is no longer capable of engendering a national policy with regard to economic production or distribution. Crucial economic decisions concerning the development of new markets, worker retraining, the applications of new technology, and, ultimately, distributional equity simply cannot be encouraged by a government structured to serve officeholders and their private-interest constituencies.

Given the destructured, impotent public domain that now exists along with all of the preconstitutional imbalances described earlier, a public officeholder's involvement with those private economic interests that best ensure his or her individual incumbency has become almost inevitable. In this climate, governmental protection of economically unproductive, distributionally distorted but politically sacrosanct private institutions is fostered by a governmental inability to assemble the public will to address the country's problems. This lack of consideration for the public well-being, reflected in the excessively short-term manner in which key economic decisions have been made in recent years, can only be remedied by an enhanced public oversight of those decisions concerning the financial and human capital that the private domain must invest to reinvigorate the American economy.

Although it would be an error to charge the government with the active management of the vast American economy in any detailed way, broad-gauge investment strategies, designed to counter international competition and at the same time ensure the well-being of the American employee who is constantly losing employment opportunities to foreign workers, must be encouraged by the government. All developed nations that compete with the United States possess governmental institutions that can, at the least, ensure minimally effective productive and minimally just distributive policies. Only the United States government—as originally constituted to some degree, but more particularly as it has become restructured in recent years—is unable to provide such a basic level of assistance to its private institutions.

Recently, the nation's need for increased productivity and enhanced global competitiveness has placed the national government under pressure to consider remedies for economic stagnation and inequity. Some reformers have suggested a return to decentralized economic structures—a weighing-in against the pure size of America's corporations. Advocates of this remedy point out that an increasing share of American employment is being claimed by midsize and smaller enterprises. What they fail to recognize, however, is that globally competitive corporations will be held to a world standard that will inevitably mandate considerable economies of scale. At least in some economic arenas, this standard will necessitate larger, not smaller, productive units. It would be a false reform to fragment American industries at a time when they must compete more vigorously than ever with large productive units from abroad.

But in return for public acquiescence to productively advantageous mergers, acquisitions, and, perhaps, the crossing of sensitive business jurisdictions such as those between banking and investment, the private-to-public balance must be adjusted so as to ensure prudent investment and worker protection during this transitional period. Acquisitions that are nonproductive or that strain debt availability, as well as such nonproductive investment strategies as those provided by the options markets, arbitrage strategies, and the like, impede rather than improve both economic productivity and distributional equity. The acceptance of an international standard of corporate size and structure carries a deeper, not shallower, public responsibility to invest wisely and to distribute productive gains in an equitable manner.

A new-found economic competitiveness, even if it is based on a partial relaxation of traditional American standards of antitrust regulation, must simultaneously encourage a commitment from American-based corporations to employ America's workers. As the global economy has progressed toward fully integrated international markets, other countries increasingly have required their economic institutions to refrain from unduly exporting employment. The United States government—again, in large part because of the growing influence of private interests on office-holders—has done a far less satisfactory job of protecting the jobs of American workers.

Far more than most Americans would like to think, America's position in the global economy is in some respects returning to

what it was at the beginning of the Republic. As overseas debts
increase and as entire domestic industries and their employments
leave America's shores, more and more products are available
only from abroad. The burden of a growing private and public
debt that increasingly is assumed by foreign governments and
investors has compounded the federal deficit with imbalances of
private trade and international debt. The ability of foreign national interests, both public and private, either to purchase American interests and move them offshore or force American
companies to expatriate so many American jobs in order to maintain competitive cost levels has meant that lower-paying occupations have found it easier to survive in the United States while
better-paying jobs have left. This unhealthy trend has corre-
sponded directly to the willingness of America's private management to ignore the long-term costs of considering the world's
workers as indistinguishable from our own. That willingness, in
turn, hinges on the ability of the American government to reconstitute itself in ways that will further consideration of just such
costs. The return of structural coherence to the national government would, without question, contribute to the government's
ability to convey the nation's interest in the continued employment of its citizens in America's economic institutions.

The Next Challenge

For all of the similarities between America's present uncompeti-
tive position and the position of the embryonic national economy
of 200 years ago, there are two fundamental differences, apart
from the nation's still enormous relative wealth, between where
America is now and where it was then. At the time of our
nation's founding, pure economic necessity required a mercantil-
istic commitment to building and maintaining the roads, canals,
ports, and harbors that would support a private economy in an

emerging nation. Today, however, with plenty rather than scarcity dominating our collective memory, such a commitment to a balanced private-public partnership is lacking.

Secondly, our decline in international standing has come at a time at which the reciprocity of America's private and public domains, even apart from their balance or imbalance, is less discussed then ever—far less, certainly, than at the time of the nation's founding. As the nation has increasingly bestowed legal immunity on the management of private economic institutions and as it has granted an extraordinary level of insulation to private management, public discussion of the human, financial, and infrastructural cost to the nation of this immunity and insulation has diminished accordingly.

Whenever possible, of course, the role of the public domain in the private economic endeavor should be supportive. But before the public and private domains can be rebalanced, their inherently reciprocal nature must first be understood and debated by the American people. If the private domain is to stand for the long-term well being of this nation, as America's fledgling economic institutions did in the nation's early years, a modern transcendence of the public/private divide in the quest for America's greater good must be achieved now, much as it was achieved then.

The reason that the necessary political debate over this issue has not taken place to date is simple: private economic institutions have been permitted to extend their domain within the American economy to the halls of influence in the United States government. These institutions have been permitted to protect those who have worked too comfortably for too long within a private domain that is undisciplined by competitive markets, and by an American citizenry that has been taught to be all too skeptical of the public domain.

As noted above, corporate management has benefited from

this tolerance with a greater level of personal legal protection and a lower level of governmental oversight than has existed at any time since the late nineteenth century. Whether or not such a high level of legal protection has been justified in the past, freedom from public responsibility while shepherding the American economy through a period more perilous than any since the country's founding is no longer a wise course of action.

America's material and capital assets are more extended and less adequate to the task of international competition than they have been since the early days of the Republic. The same is true of our human assets: the capabilities of our work force relative to those of other nations have declined markedly in the past years, one-fifth of our adult population, for example, not being able to read at even a sixth-grade level. The United States will not recover its former position in the global economy until it husbands its material and its human resources and provides for timely additions to them.

The privilege of conducting private business in the freest economic and political climate in the world carries the largest, not the smallest, obligation to conduct that business in the public interest. The antifederalists, in contrast to the federalists, were aware of potential derelictions of the private duty, even if they could not have foreseen how the government would be altered to further such derelictions. The task of balancing the public domain with the private domain has always been a proper one for the American government. But in order to assure that the balances and reciprocities between the private and public domains are renewed, America's government must be reconstituted so that it will be equal to the task of encouraging its private domain to do nothing less than what is best for the country.

In the United States, private industry has prospered through what have been less than fully competitive national and international markets. In the nation's third century, those markets will be more competitive still. The extent to which the United States can sustain and improve its productive capacity, as well as afford its working citizenry opportunity and security, is directly related to the extent to which America's government ensures its own political well-being. To strengthen our economic and political positions in the world, in short, we must first strengthen our government. Second, we must use our government in the way the federalists to some degree and the antifederalists to an even greater degree insisted that we do. We must restructure our government in such a way that it is able to do what is best for both America's economic well-being and America's democracy.

3

The Washington Beltway

Origin and Purpose

Any discussion of the recent alterations in the American government must include the growth of those ancillary institutions that encircle the government more certainly than ever before. The Beltway consultant is one such institution. Although the Beltway that surrounds the District of Columbia is only twenty years old, what goes on around it is now very much a part of the government.

The Beltway was built to divert an ever-growing volume of vehicular traffic away from the center of the city of Washington. In that regard, it has been successful. Also in part because of the construction of the Washington rail transit system, the traffic arteries in the Washington metropolitan area are at least manageable now for the resident commuter and the tourist alike. Sadly, however, the Beltway symbolically has transcended its intended role of traffic diversion; it now stands for a real diversion from the original design of the government.

Built to assist the city by ensuring that its public function was not hampered by difficult access, the Beltway has, ironically, ringed the city in a way that has retarded the access of the people to their government. To get to Washington physically, one must cross the Beltway. To get to Washington metaphorically—in the sense of securing a fair hearing before the government—increasingly the public must also cross the Beltway. The Beltway is no longer exclusively a roadway for travelers. It has also become a resting place, a permanent home really, for entrenched political consultants who have secured an intimate relationship to the government while isolating the citizenry from it.

Other American cities have traffic beltways ringing their metropolitan areas for the same purposes that Washington's Beltway was built. The impact of these beltways has lately been the subject of much study and these studies have suggested that, more often than not, beltways have drained the economic life out of the center city. Worse, they have had an adverse impact on that subtle but important sense of local community that holds a metropolis together. A sense of community is something that any people who have a common referent and a common stake in their mutual fortune should have. Beltways around America's cities have exacted a cost well in excess both of the loss of the taxable land that they use or the decline in the value of the land in the downtown areas they encircle. Beltways have almost invariably divided their cities.

Preconstitutional Conditions

The existence of the Washington Beltway, with the accompanying establishment of lucrative, government-related enterprises along it, has made a considerable difference in how the government operates within the Beltway's ten-mile radius. To understand how the Beltway has changed our government, we must digress for a brief discussion of that second preconstitutional balance that underpinned the American constitutional order. We must briefly review the origins and the current status of the balance between America's legal and political domains. Any understanding of how this balance, or imbalance, came to be what it is today must include an understanding of what that balance was at the time of the Constitutional Convention.

The richest legacy of the Anglo-Saxon legal and political tradition is the concept of the legal domain. Even in victory, the Norman kings were mindful of the difficulty of imposing a novel legal order on those whom they had conquered. They settled for what were called *assizes*—"sittings"—in which the private law was regularized into what became the English common law. Founded on the existing private institutions of property and contract, the common law ensured that the English yeoman could carry on his daily obligations without petition to the government. Over the years, the common law evolved considerably, that evolution being accepted by the government as it extended its protection throughout England. Even those statutes designed to perfect the relationship of property and contract, such as the 1677 Statute of Frauds, were more often evidentiary than substantive. They rarely changed English property or contract-based law in any fundamental way.

The evolution of the English common law, along with that of democratic public institutions in England, was uneven, to be sure. But the law and the principles of government that followed it were common to the people. They dealt with the people as an aggregate, a whole. The citizenry was thus to be governed, whether by law or by government, as a universal, governable people. The most formidable modern resistance to the evolution of the English common law came from the Stuarts, specifically during the debate over the prerogatives of the Crown vis-à-vis those of the aspiring Parliament and the newly robust mercantile class. Though often subtly stated, the debate between the new mercantilists and the Parliament on the one hand and the Stuarts on the other was really over the sanctity of the private law. The importance of that sanctity was absolutely central, of course, to the principal argument for the continued expansion of Parliament's prerogatives, specifically the extension of the rule of law. English law, recall, was still largely private, not legislative, at that time, as it had been since its origins.

It was only because of their positive experience with the private common law, and particularly because of the law's self-regulatory equities and its self-generating adaptations to modernity, that the English so readily accept politically made parliamentary law. The traditional understandings concerning that law, as they related to the increasing power of the Parliament and as they were made even clearer by John Locke at the close of the seventeenth century, made it imperative that Parliament never vitiate the rule of law in what all still recognized as an overwhelmingly private, legally ordered society.

Inherent in the position of Edward Coke, John Locke, and other seventeenth-century parliamentary advocates was another profound concept—one just as important for the development of English democracy as the concept of private law. The new democrats were, at least minimally, prepared to advocate political representation, with Coke's position (far more so than Locke's, incidentally) being that public institutions could ably alter the public order because such alterations would most likely be in keeping with the well-established principles of English law.

To be sure, English limitations of the degree to which the public should be empowered to engage in legislation, in the sense that Coke anticipated, were real indeed. The common-law roots of the English parliamentary movement ensured that the emergingly democratic Parliament would be restrained in its intrusions on personal liberties. But within the prescribed arena of concerns that were adjudged to require public consideration, the great English contribution to democracy was that an ever-growing portion of the public could participate in the consideration of how the nation would address its modernity.

To reiterate: the intellectual roots of the early English definition of political democracy lay in the deep English respect for the common law and the law's inherent resistance to the Crown's invasion of both legal and political liberties. The origins of English democracy, therefore, can be traced to a *private*, essentially *legal* domain that was, ironically by today's understanding, *collective* in its political form rather than individualistic. The limitations on public government that Locke and other late-seventeenth-century mercantile thinkers encouraged relied foundationally upon the well-bonded nature of this private, legal jurisdiction.

Less than 100 years after Locke's death, the Framers at the American Constitutional Convention, as well as the delegates to each state's ratifying conventions, vigorously debated the unique arrangements of an even more public government than the English government of the seventeenth century. The wisdom of the separation of legislative and executive powers, the singularity and tenure of the executive powers, the weaving of an intricate web of checks and balances between and among all of the government's powers were argued and reargued up and down the land.

Underlying those arguments—indeed, underlying the comfort with which such intensely political discussions could be held—was a firm understanding over the proper balance between not only the private and the public domains but the legal and political domains as well. It should never be forgotten that the hard-won acceptance of America's new public arrangement was conditioned on an unwritten, but extraordinarily important, compromise regarding the proper degree of democratic, public involvement in the average American's life. By then, the legal protections that the federalists were most concerned with preserving in the new American order were far more individualistic in their political direction.

The role of the federalists in the crafting of a government that did not threaten the private "rights of Englishmen" has been universally overstated. Yes, the original seven articles of the Constitution, in a sense created in response to General Henry Knox's overblown report to George Washington about Daniel Shays's rebellion, were designed to protect the private, legal domain, and they vigorously did so. But these original seven articles—written by men of property, not by men who preferred the political democracy that some states had already claimed—would not have been ratified but for the consent of another group of citizens who were, frequently, considerable private figures themselves but who were more sympathetic to the *collective* private sphere that had been the essence of the common law in the previous century.

Simply stated, the compromise that ensured the ratification of the Constitution—the compromise that was primary to this nation's founding and its acceptance of the convention's formal agreements—was the compromise that resulted in the Bill of Rights. It is not well taught in America's schools that the Bill of Rights was not the creation of the federalist Framers of the Constitution, and it is even more poorly taught that the Bill of Rights was the product of those who originally opposed the Constitution. It was the antifederalists, the Constitution's opponents, who insisted upon what were originally twelve but eventually became the ten guarantees of *public, political* liberties that soon accompanied the Constitution's formal governmental design.

Unfortunately, the liberties that the Bill of Rights ensures are most frequently represented as *individual* rights—rights that secure the sanctity of individual citizens in their relationship to the general government. In one way, of course, they *are* individual rights, in the sense that they reside, they have their *locus*, in whomever they would protect. But more importantly, they are political rights that are decidedly not individual in the *purpose* of the protection that they offer. The Bill of Rights' purpose is to assure a means of aggregative, democratic participation in government, much as the common law had assured an aggregative participation of private citizens in the law of the seventeenth century and before in the development of English democracy. This distinction is nowhere more relevant than in the First Amendment protections of (1) freedom of religion, (2) freedom of speech, (3) freedom of the press, (4) freedom of association, and (5) freedom to petition the government. But the true nature of these protections is frequently misunderstood.

With regard to the first of those protections, the freedom of religion, the *locus* and the *telos* of the freedom are much the same. Religious freedom, born out of the experiences of the Puritans, the Huguenots, and other religiously persecuted immigrants, wrapped around the private citizen, protecting that individual's right to practice, or not to practice, a very private belief. The other freedoms of the first amendment, however, are wholly different in form from freedom of religion. Although the origin of these rights—or, better, the origin of the protections that maintain each as a right—is private, the purpose of each is public. The freedoms of speech, press, assembly, and petition are all *aggregational* in their political direction; they all encourage the coming together of a public to debate and decide issues of common importance. Historically, the provisions of the Bill of Rights that protect individual citizens from judicial overzealousness were a reaction to such practices as the Star Chamber and trial-by-ordeal practices of courts that were created by those English monarchs who wished to stifle political dissent. That dissent, although again private in origin, was collective in its form. It was emergingly democratic and dealt with what the dissenters from the Crown believed to be the general good.

In its essence, then, there is no more important understanding of the Bill of Rights than that which clearly designates this extraordinary addition to the American Constitution as a collective and not an individualistic package of liberties. The Bill of Rights assumes within itself the all-encompassing nature of the common law that once resided exclusively in the private domain and that was carried over into the public domain as England, and later the United States, became essentially democratic polities. The antifederalists were afraid that America had, above all, lost the English momentum toward public, democratic government in the Philadelphia Constitution of 1787. They feared that the antimajoritarian structure of the new government would deprive them of their public rights as citizens because the first seven articles of the Constitution would make majoritarian attempts at public lawmaking far more difficult than they thought such attempts should be. The antifederalists' Bill of Rights essentially sought to assure in the United States what the antifederalists thought that the aggregative, private will of the common law had assured in England.

Although it is not often thought of in this way, the antifederalist position on the original seven articles of the Constitution more closely approximated the political position of Edward Coke in its upholding of political rights than it did the position of John Locke in its upholding of property rights. So, too, it was the Cokeian antifederalists, not the Lockeian federalists, who fostered the evolution of modern popular government in the American experience by ensuring the existence of public lawmaking and the requisite airing of those public issues that require democratic lawmaking. The antifederalists did so, however, by openly preferring the aggregative political purpose of the common-law tradition to the individualistic, contractual form of the private law. Again, the so-called individual protections of the First Amendment were and still are individual only in the *locus* of their legal enforceability by individuals: that is they are individual only in that the privilege of exercising each right is protected through individually generated legal guarantees. Within a *political* context, however, the guarantees are, as the antifederalists properly understood them, public and democratic. They were intended to be far different from the guarantees of public access that were provided by the original seven articles of the Constitution alone and, to end our digression, from the guarantees of public access to the government that are now restricted by institutions such as the Washington Beltway.

The Beltway and the City

Any thorough analysis of the democratic nature of the American constitutional order, and particularly of its current private-to-public and legal-to-political balances, must include the role of the Beltway and the other ancillary Washington institutions in the alteration of America's unwritten constitution. The Beltway consultant is just that—a consultant. He or she is an independent source of information who responds to a singular, private interest seeking information that can be used to influence the general government. The Beltway consultants, operating in proximity to a government that invites and increasingly requires reliance upon the consultant's services, have not only singularized the private interest; they have also altered the delicate balance between private and public influences that must be maintained in a democratic government. To place the matter in the context of the original constitutional debate, the consultant has altered that balance in favor of the antimajoritarian, federalist position, as opposed to the majoritarian, antifederalist position. To understand that alteration better now requires an analysis of the current status of our fourth preconstitutional balance, the balance of the centrifugal, as opposed to the centripetal, structures of the American government.

Insofar as the constitutional structure of the American government, like that of all institutions to some degree, reflected a balance between integrative and nonintegrative, or centripetal and centrifugal forces, it was the Bill of Rights, and particularly the First Amendment freedoms as drafted by the antifederalists, that responded to the need for structural cohesiveness by providing for public, majoritarian influence on the government. But as Alexis de Tocqueville and other observers of the American political system noted as early as the 1830s, influences on democratic government were already beginning to favor the form of singular, usually economically driven, demands advocated by what Tocqueville labeled voluntary associations and what we would today call interest groups.

The structural balance between a citizenry's right to petition the government in the form of a majoritarian, or aggregative, plea and its right to petition in the form of an individual plea, is analogous to the government's own balance between centrifugal and centripetal institutional forces. Just as the government was designed to reconcile individual and majoritarian claims in order to achieve the general good, so too it was designed to maintain a balance between the centripetal and centrifugal forces of its own structure. For a time, these structural balances were reasonably well maintained in the American governmental order, even though the Framers' attention to this balance in their government was surely more intuitive than explicit.

But if individual interests and majoritarian interests did share governmental favor more or less equally for a time, it is clear that today one form of governmental access dominates the other. The individual, Tocquevilleian form of influence that comes from, say, a particular economic interest now clearly overwhelms the majoritarian form of influence that grows out of a public need for improved education, heightened environmental protection, and the like.

One of the principal reasons for the ascendance of the individual over the aggregative form of governmental influence within the national government is the existence of the Washington Beltway, for it is the Beltway, often in place of the government, that now supplies expertise to so many privately advocated actions that compete for public favor. As the Beltway has marketed that expertise for individual hire, the Tocquevilleian, individual form of influence on the government carried the day over the majoritarian forms of Washington influence that the antifederalists supported.

A second result of this uneven federalist/antifederalist balance has recently placed an even greater burden upon the government. Just as the Framers did not understand how the balance between different forms of petition to the government might be altered over time, they did not understand how an alteration in the balance of the forms of influence on the government might cause a restructuring of the government itself. The Framers could not foresee, in other words, how the private purveyor of governmental expertise, along with the public officeholder who is beholden to such expertise, would over time bend the governmental order to best accommodate the interests of both that officeholder and those individuals who would influence the government through singular channels such as the Beltway.

Again, it is the *form* of the interaction between the Beltway consultant and the institutional arrangements of the government that is of primary importance here. Just as the existence of a beltway in other cities has affected how those cities have gone about their business, Washington's Beltway consultants have affected the *form* of how it is that the government must deal with the nation's public business. The very existence of the relatively new form of access to governmental favor embodied in the Beltway consultant bespeaks a government and a generation of officeholders that have overwhelmingly adopted the Tocquevilleian method of nonaggregated, historically federalist access to the government over the aggregated, antifederalist forms of access. And, as the Beltway has encouraged highly individual, or non-aggregative, forms of access to the detriment of majoritarian influence, the government has increasingly restructured itself in order to receive the private petition that best suits the individualistic form. The government, with the approval if not the encouragement of the officeholder, has thus become an increasingly centrifugal structure, a structure it must assume in order to receive the individualistic form of petition more easily.

The Triumph of the Private Domain

One final governmental change has resulted from the rise of the Washington Beltway consultant. If one of the most important preconditions for a democratic government is that of a healthy balance between its public-to-private and its legal-to-political domains, then the recent impact of the Washington Beltway consultant must also be weighed in terms of its impact upon these balances.

Both the English in the seventeenth century and the American Framers in the eighteenth century were keenly aware of the need to balance the private and public domains. Both countries sought to protect the private prerogatives of people who insisted on the freedom to go about their daily lives largely unimpeded by the government. Once again, however, the guarantee of that private freedom required, and also underpinned, the granting of public and increasingly democratic political powers to a government whose powers flowed historically from the collective, although private, tradition of the common law. As a result, both the English and the American political experiences permitted a gradual and healthy extension of the political jurisdiction of public institutions. The creators of the British Bill of Rights, like the antifederalist creators of the American Bill of Rights, were concerned above all with the public's right to petition its government in politically majoritarian ways.

It is not too much to say that the exclusive placing of the Beltway consultant's singularizing expertise into the increasingly private channels of the government has meant that the Beltway consultant has gone a long way toward the reversal of this process and has thus accelerated the triumph of the private over the public domain in American politics. Not only because the true nature of the Beltway's business is so overwhelmingly private, but also because the form of the Beltway's business has had such an impact on the form of the public's institutions, the imbalancing of America's public-to-private domains has now been radically advanced.

The Washington Beltway, in doing nothing less than removing the government's sources of information from the government's own center, has seriously impaired the government's ability to deal with complex public issues. The balances struck by the federalists and the antifederalists over 200 years ago between the private interests of individual citizens and the public interests of the citizenry as a whole have surely been distorted. The resulting imbalance between the forms of influence that impact on the American government, in part brought about by the Beltway's singularization of public issues, has assisted in the de-democratization of the American government.

4

The Lawyer-Lobbyist

Legal and Political Jurisdictions

America's constitutional design purposely accentuated the role of law, both in the private and in the public domain. America was to be a government of law, and the balance of institutional powers struck in the first seven articles of the Constitution was adopted by the Framers in order to protect the guarantees of law from the excesses of political power. As noted in the preceding chapter, that balance between legal and political jurisdictions was in a sense rebalanced by the Bill of Rights from the side of political majoritarianism. That resulting larger balance has been disrupted seriously in recent years. This is a development that is as dangerous as it is unexamined.

The typical study of America's legal and political balances focuses on the jurisdictional separations among America's political branches. The protection of more or less sovereign institutional arenas is important, to be sure. But there is a good deal more to the relationship of law and politics in the American national government than institutional prerogatives protect.

Though there have been intrusions of one jurisdiction on another, legal and political, throughout American history, the institutions that reflect the legal and political domains of America's constitutional order have complemented each other rather well. As law was to be paramount, the legal protections of rights were purposely well-secured in a government that would assure such rights. The antifederalists, in seizing upon the majoritarian political implications of the common law, led the federalists to seize upon the legal protections of those individual rights that were property related in the first instance. In an attempt to assuage the fears of the antifederalists and to promote the Philadelphia Constitution's restrictions on government, Alexander Hamilton argued that the Supreme Court would always be "the least dangerous branch." But while Hamilton downplayed the likelihood of Supreme Court intrusion into the political jurisdiction, he also crafted the argument for the judicial review of legislated law. The antifederalists were rightly suspicious.

Throughout the history of the Republic, the boundary between the legal and political jurisdictions has moved freely. Chief Justice John Marshall was not above stretching the rules of legal construction in order to place Hamilton's *Federalist* argument for judicial review directly into *Marbury* v. *Madison*. After Marshall's lengthy tenure as Chief Justice, his successor, Roger Taney, moved back toward granting legislated law greater leeway during most of his tenure. But even Taney surely intruded on the political jurisdiction in his notorious, pre–Civil War *Dred Scott* ruling about the nonexistence of a federal right to citizenship.

The late-nineteenth-century Supreme Court negated federal and state legislation frequently. It did so in order to protect an exaggerated notion of private property and contract. The early 1930s witnessed much the same kind of intrusion until Chief Justice Charles Evans Hughes retipped the balance in favor of President Franklin Roosevelt's interventionist response to the

Great Depression. But the interplay of court and legislature, of law and politics, has not always been characterized by judicial intrusion. At times, judge-made law has filled what the courts properly considered to be a legislative void. In the absence of statutory law, the Supreme Court under Chief Justice Earl Warren expanded the rights of the accused, the rights of those denied access to a racially nonsegregated school, and the rights of those who were not fairly represented in their state legislatures and Congress.

But whether responding to legislated law or creatively substituting judicial for legislated law, the public's court has always been the institution that stands for the rule of law. Often, public reaction to judge-made law has been negative: those who were victorious in the political arena, either in the advancing of legislated law or in the forestalling of it, have argued most vehemently against what they have labeled as legal intrusions. The courts have been most robust in their judgments when they have borrowed most freely from beyond the law. Louis D. Brandeis's innovative "Brandeis brief," for example, injected the economic and social conditions of the contemporary factory worker into the early twentieth-century considerations of the Supreme Court. Justice Oliver Wendell Holmes's dissent in *Lochner* v. *New York*, which condemned the tyranny of what Holmes called "Mr. Spencer's social statics," also brought politics into the law.

Frequently, in opposition to the inclusion of political considerations in the Court's deliberations, observers have argued that the jurisdictional separation between law and politics must be guarded more carefully. Yale's Alexander Bickel, for example, has contended that the legitimacy of the Supreme Court is placed at risk when a citizenry accustomed to having its law come solely from the legislature witnesses an activist Court that disturbs that prerogative. Bickel urged judicial restraint in all of his writings, frequently citing Hamilton and the need for the courts to remain "the least dangerous branch."

The federalist drafters of the first seven articles of the Constitution, advocates of the courts as they were, expected those courts to protect the substantive rights, and particularly the property rights, that they held dear. They were content to permit the remainder of the government to deal with the political difficulties of the day so long as the courts would respond to any legislature's intrusions on property. The antifederalists countered that all was fair game for the legislature.

In sum, the balance between law and politics in the United States, and particularly the jurisdictional balance between the courts and Congress, has been flexible throughout the American experience. The pulling and hauling of politics and law, in the spirit of an ever-growing democracy, reflected vibrant balances among the lawmaking jurisdictions of the American system. These balances were maintained rather well throughout America's history—until recently.

The Current Imbalance

Today, a different kind of threat to the legal-to-political balance within the American governmental order has surfaced. This threat does not stem from an intrusion of either judicially created law or legislated law on the other or on the private domain. Rather, it stems from a particular *form* of practice of the *private* law before the national government—or, more specifically, from the influence that the private legal community in the nation's capital has exerted on the general government. This influence has caused a dislocation of the legal-to-political balance within the American government more severe than any jurisdictional imbalance that has been created by either the federal courts or the United States Congress.

Throughout history, many governments, democratic or not, have been influenced by ostensibly private lawyers who, in one public capacity or another, have succeeded in the overcodifying of the public law in order to bénefit from that law's arcanity. Such restriction of access to public law to legal insiders for the purpose of those insiders' personal gain is clearly unethical as well as ultimately damaging to the government. But the excessive influence of Washington lawyer-lobbyists on the American government on behalf of private clients has had a direct impact on something far more important than a limitation of access to the government's law. It has had a direct impact on the very nature of the public law. The Washington lawyer-lobbyist, in concert with those private interests that he or she represents, has done nothing less than alter the way that the American government does the public's business.

What exactly is the relationship of the Washington lawyer-lobbyist to the general government? At one level, that relationship is simply an extrapolation of the lawyer-client relationship. The relationship between a lawyer and a client is essentially contractual, and what a Washington lawyer does with the government—further a single client's private interest in the public domain—is similarly contractual in its form. Washington lawyer-lobbyists are rarely involved with requests for many-sided public policies; equally rarely are they advocates of a general perspective on broad-based public policies. The usual request made upon government by a private interest through a Washington lawyer-lobbyist is only singular in nature. Accordingly, it carries the form of the private contract into the public government.

Of course, all private interests, whether individual or aggregated into a majoritarian form, are guaranteed the right to petition the government. But, as with the Beltway consultant, the recent onslaught of singular petitions to the national government has had an impact on the way that the government does the public's business. When singular, contractual forms of political advocacy outbalance majoritarian requests for public policy, the government naturally is forced to respond disproportionately to the former form of request. Together with the Washington Beltway consultant, then, the Washington lawyer-lobbyist has altered the balance of centrifugal-to-centripetal forces in the government. And he or she has done so within the letter of the formal Constitution. The American government is now doing business on more of a contractual basis than it has ever done before—and more than it was ever intended to do.

How, specifically, has this alteration in the structural balances of the United States government been precipitated by those who lobby for private clients? As described before, the balance of law and politics in the United States has historically been sustained by the relative balance of influence among the branches of the constitutional government. The governmental branches have typically maintained their institutional prerogatives by claiming and reclaiming jurisdictional territory as the sway of politics over time permitted them to do so. But insofar as political interests in the larger society balanced or, temporarily, imbalanced the legal and political branches of the government, those interests have also directed their influence indiscriminately through whichever branch of the government offered the most promise of governmental favor. When one governmental branch overstepped another in claiming to do the public's business, the branch that was intruded upon could rely, over time, on support from an active public in its attempt to recapture lost ground.

In that way, the judicial excesses of the Supreme Court—in defense of the private domain at the end of the last century or in remedying the legislative deficiencies of Congress in the pre–civil rights period, for example—were not only countered substantively by the opposing branch; they were countered jurisdictionally as well, by a return to a balance between the jurisdictions that receive the public's pleas for justice. The beneficiaries of school integration in the *Brown* v. *The Board of Edu-*

cation case, (one of the two cases, *Baker* v. *Carr* being the other, cited by the late Chief Justice Warren as the most important of his tenure), upheld the institutional prerogatives of the Court as well as the plaintiff's pleas for justice. Even if those pleas may, in turn, have temporarily altered the balance among the institutions of the government, they did not alter the balance between the far more fundamental legal and political forms, or between the contractual and aggregative forms, of governmental decision making.

The Washington lawyer-lobbyist, on the other hand, has immeasurably altered the *forms* of access to the legislative branch of the government, and in doing so has gravely diminished the democratic nature of the government. For the Washington lawyer-lobbyist, in pleading the interests of private, singular clients before the government, has advanced those interests not through the judicial branch of the government, where individual claims have historically been heard, but through Congress and, to a lesser extent, the executive branch of the government. Thus, the Washington lawyer, unlike a lawyer who truly practices the law, has artificially forced the singular form of the law, the contractual form, into what should be the aggregative structures of Congress.

The simple fact is that contrary to the practice of everyday legal advocacy, which typically represents clients either in a court of law or in settlements that anticipate and thus avoid a court of law, Washington lawyer-lobbyists spend little time before the nation's courts and focus their activities on congressional committees and staff. The unbalanced use of those points of access in the government has had a direct impact on the balance between the legal and political domains in the government. Not surprisingly, as Congress has more and more fallen under the influence of the Washington lawyer-lobbyist, it has increasingly become incapable of aggregating public policy. Like a court, or like two lawyers who anticipate a court, it has become an institution that deals with the nation's business only in a contractual, legalistic form.

Another Private-Public Imbalance

Once again, however, the imbalance between the legal and the political domains in the United States government is not the most significant product of the Washington lawyer-lobbyist's influence. even more important is the fact that the Washington lawyer-lobbyist's influence has perverted the government by increasingly restricting access to the government to the contractual form. To put it another way, the singular claim of the lawyer-assisted private interest, as opposed to the majoritarian claim for an overall perspective on governmental policy, has now so overwhelmed the government that the government is increasingly capable of receiving only the contractual, legal form of petition in its daily procedures. Again, contrary to the appropriate professional role of the private lawyer who represents private clients in a court of law, the Washington lawyer-lobbyist, in effect, practices law before the political branches of the government and their previously balanced transactional and aggregative decision processes. By practicing law before the legislature and not before the courts, the Washington lawyer-lobbyist has redesigned the form of access to the government—and the unwritten constitution in the bargain.

Citing a traditional standard of democracy, of course, Washington lawyer-lobbyists would argue that their task is to facilitate democratic representation before the national government. As all citizens and all groupings or interests within the citizenry have the right to petition their government, all citizens, at least formally, are entitled to employ whoever best assists them in that representation. But as the use of ostensibly private lawyers to assist singular private interests to gain public representational favor has resulted in the overwhelming adoption of the legal form within the government as a whole, the form of private law, as an interceder for individual interests, has supplanted the form of public law within the government and particularly within the jurisdictional balance between the courts and the legislature that is necessary to the survival of American democracy.

The rise of the Washington lawyer-lobbyist has led to one more alteration of the government: a structural elongation of the informal government under which the Washington lawyer-lobbyist, like the Beltway consultant, is now someone who is more within than without the government. The inclusion of the Washington lawyer-lobbyist within the government, needless to say, has not improved the representativeness of the government. Rather, as in the case of the Washington Beltway consultant, it has thrown up another barrier to democracy that the citizenry, as it expresses itself in the majoritarian tradition, needs to cross in order to gain access to its government. The new influence of the Washington lawyer-lobbyist is thus one more reason why the American government is less democratic today than it has been since its earliest days. The lawyer-lobbyists' extension of the national government to their own offices in Washington, in short, impedes the representational function that the United States government, like any democratic government, must provide for its citizenry.

5

The Elections Industry

The Original Design

A third collection of ancillary figures has found a way to make itself essential to the workings of the American federal government. The Washington-based elections industry, if it has done nothing else, has surely contributed to, and taken advantage of, the enormous changes that have taken place in the manner of electing America's national officeholders. Within the framework of what is still, if somewhat more tenuously than in the past, a democratic method of election, the American political system now selects both its executive and its legislative leaders in a way that largely depends on the Washington elections industry.

Most of the contemporary criticism of our government's changed election processes has centered around the enormous increase in the cost of running for national office. Surely, that increase signals that there is something unhealthy about America's political system. Many capable citizens are prevented from running for public office, while less worthy citizens continue to serve solely because they have the resources to do so.

Monetary constraints on running for office, however, are only a symptom of something more worrisome about America's electoral processes. The manner of selecting our officeholders has changed in a way that both reflects and contributes to fundamental changes in our political system. It is the manner in which a citizen runs for and holds public office today that has changed so thoroughly.

Throughout history, all politicians have had patrons and protectors, advocates and friends. Few public figures, even the holders of relatively minor local offices, have ever attained their positions without the assistance of others. In democratic political systems, the importance of political supporters has not diminished; in fact, it may have increased. For one thing, public acceptability of an officeholder must surely be broader in a democracy than in authoritarian political systems. One of the constraints that a democratic public places on its officeholders is that because many must consent to the accession to the office, many must be represented by the officeholder. Appropriately, many should also be heard, it is argued, when governance begins following a democratic election.

But certain relationships of supporters to officeholders, even in a democracy, can be excessive. Surely, the donation of large sums of money to a candidate by one or a small number of supporters undermines democratic representation by encouraging such officeholders to respond more readily to those few who directly assisted them in gaining office. In the past, the United States government has surely suffered from the biases of officeholders who were beholden to only a few citizens or interests.

In response to increasingly credible charges that a few citizens possessed an inordinate influence in America's elections, Congress in 1971 and again in 1974 adopted what it believed to be meaningful reforms of national campaign financing. Limitations were placed on the amount of money that an individual contributor could donate to candidates as well as on overall expenditures for presidential campaigns. Advocates of these reforms honestly felt that they had improved America's electoral processes and, thereby, American democracy in general. In fact, neither was improved for reasons that are easily understandable.

The relationship between the citizen and the officeholder is the most important of all democratic relationships, including the relationship of officeholders to each other. This is true even in a political system that is as structurally dispersed as America's. In seeking to distance the citizen from the officeholder, the federalists provided for indirect elections to the presidency and to the upper house of the legislature. The House of Representatives was to be selected by popular vote but, as the antifederalists properly complained, the number of representatives was too small to forestall the influence within the government of senators, a president, and a federalist court. The Seventeenth Amendment, adopted in 1913, mandated that senators be elected directly, but they were still to be apportioned evenly among the states, regardless of population. In presidential elections, the Electoral College continues to serve as the real selector of the president. Electors are not bound to the popular vote of their citizens in most states, and several have disregarded the preferences of their states' voters, most recently in the 1988 election.

Were the federalists wrong in seeking to distance the citizenry from its officeholders? Their purpose in so doing was certainly clear. Madison and others argued that the discouragement of disruptive factions in the population was essential for ordered government. But the dispersion of public passion was not designed to interrupt the functioning of government once that government was constituted. Safely distanced from the public, national officeholders were to convene in a manner that permitted equitable and effective governance. But even President George Washington, who had also served as president of the Constitutional Convention, thought it appropriate to visit the Senate and directly ask for its cooperation on a legislative matter. Although the Senate's unresponsiveness to Washington is largely depicted in the textbooks as appropriate, it is arguable that Washington was where he should have been and the Senate got it wrong.

But whatever the degree of distance between officeholders and their political jurisdictions, the standards for electoral representation in a democracy are clear. In America, within the spirit of Madison's separated powers, as in other democratic countries, two standards are more central than others. The first is substantive: that the will of the people be represented in the government. The second is procedural: that the form of democracy itself, the structure of a political system's institutions, be changed only with the approval of the citizenry.

To put it another way, a democracy must incorporate electoral processes that truly convey the public's will to the public officeholder. The result of the democratic vote, therefore, or the extension of the meaning of the vote to the place where public policy is made, is what guarantees democracy. Democracy is not assured merely by the exercise of the vote at the place of the poll.

The Framers created a balance of institutions that would at one and the same time receive the will of the public but deflect the direct will of the public as a whole. They struck what they considered to be a middle position between forcing the will of the people on the officeholder and preventing any majoritarian faction of the public either to overwhelm the government or, worse, to alter the structure of government in a way that would facilitate excessively popular government.

The Framers' technique for maintaining the above balances included a variety of political mechanisms. Not only were some offices to be filled by indirect election, but the terms of national office were made of unequal length. Most important, the branches of the government were armed with checks upon each other. The veto, the override of the veto, the processes of advice and consent on treaties and executive appointments, and other devices were all designed to ensure that no one branch of the government would overwhelm the others. Finally, limitations of age and, in the case of the president, of native birth, assured a balance of judgment and a balance between too little and too much national identity in matters of deep public concern. Beyond these restrictions, the Framers assumed a proper mixture of institutionally generated cooperation and conflict among national officeholders.

Similarly, in the manner of conducting an election for national office, the antifederalists properly assumed that the form of American elections would maintain the democratic standards of (a) referring the public will to the elected and (b) providing institutional inducements for good government. For many years, public candidates, for all of their shortcomings, were encouraged to discuss issues of general concern during the course of the campaign. In that way, candidates received, but also helped to form, a public, majoritarian will that was both evidenced by and legitimated by the election result. Once elected, officeholders were expected to represent the results of those elections within the government. The public, as in any democratic polity, has the right to believe that electoral success represents a commitment to a particular course of action.

The Representative Distortion

Lately, however, events have seriously impaired the maintenance of electoral, representative democracy in the American government. Elected officeholders less certainly represent the will of the people today because the electoral arrangement itself has been altered. Much as with the Beltway consultants and Washington's lawyer-lobbyists, not only have there been changes in the way that our national officeholders are chosen, but these changes also have helped, in turn, to alter the way in which the American government works.

This development has been fostered primarily by political candidates' tendency to engage a multitude of campaign advisers who, seeing themselves as necessary intermediaries between the electorate and the candidate, encourage the nation's candidates both to simplify and, in too many instances, to symbolically misrepresent their views on public issues. The standard of democracy, quite obviously, requires that in order to maintain a proper representation of the public will in the government, those who seek public office must, above all things, honestly and fully represent their positions on public issues. To be sure, politicians in democracies and nondemocracies alike sometimes consciously misrepresent what they plan to do once they secure public office. But what distinguishes a democracy from a nondemocracy is that prospective officeholders are held as closely as possible to their publicly stated position and that the officeholders who do not comply with their represented positions are sanctioned. Democracy's candidates, in other words, are accountable to a public record and to the matching of that public record with the positions of their campaigns.

But today, with the assistance of campaign consultants, the public positions of the prospective or incumbent national officeholder can be and frequently are both blurred and minimized, not because of the deliberate misrepresentations of office seekers that occur from time to time in democracies as well as nondemocracies, but because of the systematic intercession of the elections industry between the campaigner and the public. A distortion of the government's public, aggregative choices for policy that results from such narrowly focused campaigns necessarily follows from that intercession.

Apart from the separation between the citizenry and its government, one of the most important separations in any democracy is that between the national and the local interest. This is one of the key areas of differentiation between the general and the particular good. No political system, even an undemocratic one, can survive if it does not provide for some aggregation of its particular interests into the general good. Part of the blurring and minimizing of positions that national officeholders now practice results in the overstressing of the particular or local good at the expense of the general or national good. Elections-industry advisers, sensing the destructive potential of any deep political controversy, typically encourage candidates to speak as little as possible on national issues and as frequently as possible on local issues, or at least on the local impact of national issues, when they speak at each location in their campaign.

Also, when national issues are addressed in America's political campaigns, the political consultants advise candidates to address those issues in fragmented rather than comprehensive ways. As a result of such advice, political costs typically are not assigned to political benefits in American political campaigns, and the public is prevented from expressing preferences for alternative political options.

In sum, the elections industry itself—albeit ultimately at the behest of the officeholder who wishes to retain a position in the government—has been responsible for what amounts to an interception of the public will before it can be represented in the government. In recent elections, candidates for both houses of Congress, and even candidates for the presidency, have been able to run their campaigns on the basis of almost deliberately misleading positions on the issues of the day and to offer little or no substantive comment on matters of truly national importance.

Although constraints on direct democracy were very much a part of the Framers' constitutional design, the current wholesale avoidance of the public will transmitted to the government was never a part of the federalists', much less the antifederalists',

intention. If the conveyance to the government of the public preference upon a variety of national issues is the heart of democracy, then the American democracy, because of the intercession
of the elections industry, is not as well served today as it was
even a comparatively short time ago.

The Internal Distortion

Yet another intrusion upon American democracy, one that goes
beyond the interception of the public will, has also resulted from
the growing importance of the elections industry to the national
officeholder. Although nominally available to all office seekers,
the best of the elections industry now works almost exclusively
for incumbent officeholders. For both financial and reputational
reasons, the elections industry prefers to assist incumbents in
reelection bids. When incumbents enjoy such assistance and
challengers, largely, do not, the former hold an overwhelming
advantage in elections. This factor has changed the form of the
American government in that the government, designed as a government of private citizens who offer their services to the public,
has become a government in which the legislative officeholder,
and particularly the incumbent of the House of Representatives,
has become a nearly permanent public figure. Ninety-eight percent of incumbents who sought reelection were victorious in the
elections of 1986 and 1988. Even with considerable voter dis-
content over the budget gridlock of the 1990 congressional session and the inability of the government to deal with a variety of
other pressing national issues, ninety-six percent of incumbents
were returned in the November 1990, elections.

As a result of this near invulnerability to defeat, members of
the House no longer have a primary allegiance to either the institution of government of which they are members or to the public
at large. Their allegiance, as we have seen before, is singular in

nature and is insulated from the political influence of the general good, as well as from the general public that would represent that general good. Thus insulated, virtually all officeholders, whatever their party affiliation or regional origin, unsurprisingly have encouraged the continuation of these recent revisions of the American electoral system.

Today's electoral system, with its enormous cost and its inability to reform itself through the use of, say, public, party-directed election financing, virtually ensures the reelection of incumbents. Even the recent "reforms," designed to limit the influence of a few wealthy contributors on national elections, have only further impaired the democratic form of national election by installing the political action committee (PAC) as the primary funding mechanism for officeholders. Such a mechanism, with its direct link to particular interests, is more convenient for the officeholder and for the elections industry consultant in their joint commitment to incumbency than is any other form of funding.

It should also come as no surprise that national officeholders, particularly within Congress, do what they can to ensure the continuation of a system of public representation that, above all, protects local interests throughout the country so that those interests can reciprocally help the officeholder to be reelected. But, ironically, this mutual protection of individual interest and officeholder, within Congress particularly, only further distances the people from their government. As the officeholder develops ever tighter bonds between the few most powerful interests of an electoral district or state and his or her incumbency, the original constitutional order is increasingly distorted. That linkage does not promote any aggregative, policy-making function within a democratic government. Accordingly, it can fairly be said that no longer is it the government that governs least that governs best in the United States. It is the government that governs least, and that

therefore least imperils the governors, that best ensures undemocratic incumbencies.

The distortion of the constitutional order that has accompanied
the distortion of America's national electoral campaigns has, of
course, been a product of the unwritten revisions of the national
electoral process that have occurred at least partially at the behest
of officeholders and the Washington elections industry. Despite
the emphasis placed by many on the large number of political
groupings that now contribute to national officeholders, the representative burden has been altered not by the number of contributors but by the *form* of today's electoral contributions and the
relationship of that form of contribution to the democratic forms
of government. Although over 4,000 political action committees
now contribute to national campaigns, what is more important
than their number is that each PAC—whether it be a business
PAC, a labor PAC, or any other kind of PAC—represents only
one political interest. The singularity of that representation is
what has distorted the American political system and American
democracy.

The federalists and the antifederalists jointly designed a political system that provided for the democratic selection of public
officeholders. They also designed a system of democratic governance, even with such limitations on democracy as the indirect
election of the offices of the presidency and the Senate. In recent
years, that system has been altered in ways unforeseen by the
Framers, who feared above all the impairment of the government
by a majority of impassioned citizens. It has been the Framers'
prescribed relationship between the public and its representatives
that has been distorted by the officeholders and the elections
industry in favor of singular, disproportionately selfish interests.
The transmittal of the public will that the Framers provided for,
even with its limitations, never entailed the distortion of the public will that the current generation of officeholders has engen-

dered. Neither did the limitation of the arena for public debate that the Framers provided for within America's political institutions entail the protection of the public careers of those who now choose with impunity not to engage in such debate during the electoral period. The calculated avoidance of such debate, during both the electoral period and the period of governance, has furthered the de-democratization of America.

Redress

The last three chapters have described, and condemned, the role of the ancillary institutions of the federal government. These chapters have described how the Beltway consultant, the Washington lawyer-lobbyist, and the Washington electoral industry have altered the form of the American government as well as extended the government to include their institutions. They have also described how these alterations and these extensions have disturbed the principal preconstitutional balances of the American constitutional order.

If one thing is clear about the above institutions and the damage that they have done, it is that these institutions will not, themselves, be a part of any redress of the harm that they have caused. The problems that the ancillary institutions have brought to our government, in other words, are not self-correcting. They will need to be corrected by citizens and their constitutional institutions, working together to restore both the preconstitutional balances of the government and the constitutional effectiveness and fairness of the government.

In order to engage in that redress, some measures can be taken against the ancillary institutions themselves. The Washington lawyer-lobbyists, for example, should be regulated in such a way that they are placed on a "stand-by" or "reserve" status by respective bar associations when more than a moiety of their work involves influencing the government for private clients. Placing the individual firms of the elections industry under the control of one or the other of the political parties or placing Beltway consultants under the supervision of the congressional committees or subcommittees that are most relevant to the substance of their consultancies may, or may not, prove to be effective solutions to these two institutions' improper influence in the government as well. In a general sense, what the government must do is begin to challenge the exclusively private nature of the ancillary institutions, seeing them for the quasi-public institutions that they have become and dealing with them accordingly.

Overwhelmingly, however, redress of the excesses of Washington's ancillary institutions will come not from direct regulation or control of these institutions. Truly effective redress for the damage caused by Washington's ancillary institutions will come only through the difficult process of rebuilding and rebalancing America's nonancillary, that is governmental, institutions themselves. It is through a restoration of the appropriate pre-constitutional and constitutional balances of the government, through a re-democratization of the American government, in other words, that the government can return to being the servant of the people that Jefferson and the Framers intended. Only through a restoration of these balances will the ancillary institutions be put back into their place outside of the direct channels of governmental influence that they now occupy. That is what the government can effectively do about these institutions. How it should go about rebalancing its own institutions and how other of America's private institutions can assist in that rebalancing is what the remainder of this work will consider.

6

The Levels of Government

Aristotle and Political Identification

All but the simplest of political systems have more than one level
of government. These levels, when apportioned properly, represent different spheres of political identification or different levels
of loyalty among the citizenry. Aristotle described three levels of
political identification—those of the family, the village, and the
polity—and recommended a healthy balance among them, knowing that each contributed to an essential bonding of the citizen
with the political community.

In the modern world, the most significant structural division
among nations is the division between the unitary state and the
federal state. The unitary state rests on a uniformity, or near
uniformity, of a political culture, a national history, a language,
and the like. A federal state usually rests on a compounding of
different cultures, histories, languages, and, invariably, political
allegiances into a single polity. Natural unitary political systems
that have not unduly imposed themselves on different nationalities have an advantage over federal systems in that the focus of

their government is greater and the possibility for political divisiveness less.

The United States, from its beginnings, has been a federal state. Although there was brief consideration of the unitary form at the Philadelphia Convention, the federal nature of the national government was assured from the start, but not because of significant cultural or historical differentiations among the American people. With regard to culture and national origin, early Americans were nearly all of a kind. Only a smattering of Dutch, Huguenots, and others kept the United States from being a single, English-speaking polity at its birth. The thirteen separate British colonies that became the United States, however, became thirteen very separate states, the sovereignty of which was not questioned in either the Articles of Confederation or the 1787 Constitution.

The early history of our federal system was a mixed one. The continuation of full state sovereignty was pleasing to the antifederalists, who felt that majoritarian democracy was better protected at the level of the states than at the level of the national government. On the other hand, the continued existence of the states provided a jurisdictional cleavage from which divisions between regions, or blocs of states, could and did grow. Whether the Civil War could have been averted had the United States adopted a unitary government from the beginning can only be speculated upon. Incontrovertibly, however, the Confederacy was formed by separate states who seceded to protect what they believed to be the sovereign prerogatives of their own peoples.

States were also instrumental in the imbalances between the private interest and the public interest that developed in the latter part of the nineteenth century. Then, newly powerful private institutions used the federated nature of the general government to their advantage by postponing state protections for industrial workers, such as those afforded by the minimum wage, workers' compensation, and so forth. Even earlier, Chief Justice John Marshall, in his angry *Barron* v. *Baltimore* opinion, had ruled that federal protections in the Bill of Rights were never intended to be extended to the states.

The greatest difficulty that has resulted from the American federal structure, apart from the controversy over state sovereignty that led to the Civil War, still plagues the nation. The Framers' failure to anticipate the coming of cities, of those large, compacted communities made up of very different peoples, marked their most serious lack of foresight. The villages of the Framers' day were not much larger than those of Aristotle's time. Neither were they collections of ethnic diversity. Thinking of them in a capacity other than as creatures of their states was something that the Framers, perhaps understandably, could not and did not do.

The Urban Crisis: Its Cause

Today, America's cities represent the most profound of the nation's governmental failures. Those failures reflect, above all, an inability on the part of the national government to acknowledge fully the series of events by which the cities have gathered in themselves the most unyielding of America's problems. Not surprisingly, these problems mirror an extraordinary demographic as well as ethnic diversity, for it is in the cities that the old and the young, the poor, and the greatest collection of America's minorities huddle amongst fortified pockets of a well-to-do urban citizenry. Equally unsurprising is the fact that it is in the cities that the education provided by public primary and secondary schools is of the least value.

The governmental roots of this crisis are not hard to isolate. If the Framers did not anticipate cities, which are now the primary intermediate level of political identification, the states further complicated matters by designating the county as their principal

subdivision. That modern cousin of the English shire is still re-
ferred to in textbooks as the area that could be patrolled by a
mounted constabulary between the rising and setting of the sun.
In America's greater cities, such as New York, Chicago, and Los
Angeles, and even in many of its midsized cities, the county
jurisdiction has long detracted from the natural political identity
of the area. Counties, a rural concept, belie the political identification of the village, as Aristotle understood it, in the American
democracy.

The longstanding political battles between cities, particularly
major cities, and their states are not accidental either. Beyond
their early role in the negation of a federal standard of civil
liberties and their later role in the denial of economic equity, the
states historically and purposefully discriminated against their
own cities in ways that have seriously harmed the country. Underlying this discrimination was the states' fear not only of the
accelerated growth of cities in the latter portion of the nineteenth
century, but also of the immigration to those cities of populations
that were in large part neither northern nor western European. In
the early years of this century, states that contained large and
diverse cities employed three strategies of discrimination against
the cities. Some state governments, such as those of New York
and Illinois, passed laws that severely restricted their cities' ability to annex territory. In this way, large cities that heretofore had
easily moved their corporate limits in keeping with the dispersion
of their populations were prevented from any further claim of
citizenship on those who selfishly had moved beyond their borders. That, of course, was the idea.

The second type of discriminatory state legislation facilitated
the granting of separate municipal charters to even the smallest
collections of citizens who had lately moved beyond the city's
borders. Not content with providing a legal demarcation to protect recent escapees from the cities' jurisdictional reach, the dom-

inant rural interests in many state legislatures sought to protect their political majorities in the legislature by providing corporate havens for the new emigrants. The suburbs that soon encircled each of America's major cities stand today as the principal barrier to an intermediate political identity in America. The modern metropolitan area, in spite of its size, is the true analog of Aristotle's village, but because of the in-state suburb—and in the case of New York City because of the out-of-state suburb—these areas are politically divided and politically underrepresented within their states. And they must compete politically with those who should be a part of them.

A final disabling discrimination completed the trio of state strategies against their own cities. Also at the turn of the century, states routinely violated their own constitutions by failing to reapportion their legislatures after the decennial censuses. State legislatures, already overrepresenting their rural areas in upper houses, which were apportioned on the basis of area, soon disproportionately represented rural areas in their lower houses as well. The federal nature of the American political arrangement, until the intercession of the Supreme Court in the 1960s, prevented the remedying of this underrepresentation. Ironically, when the Court did speak to the misrepresentation, the balance of population within the metropolitan areas (largely because of the impact of the other two discriminations) had been irretrievably altered. The Court's legal decision failed to redress the political injustice, and its tardy call to representative equity, ironically, benefited those who had moved to the suburbs, not those who had remained in the city.

The Urban Crisis: The Result

The modern result of the historical, structurally facilitated biases against America's great cities is clear. As America's cities have become refuges for the disadvantaged, they have also become the places where the benefits of private employment, privately financed housing, private health care, and other necessary human services are least available. And, largely because of the federated nature of the American government, the city has become the place where the public remedy for these private disadvantages was also the least available. As a result, the great cities of America have become, perhaps irreversibly, home to the greatest levels of crime, of unemployment, and of homelessness.

A city could not be more different politically from a rural area or a town. It is a place for either the fulfillment of that human complexity that can come from the commingling of different peoples or for the decay and disassembling of all that commingling once meant to those who moved there. It can be a place where the best of a nation's culture and the best of a nation's creativities propel the nation's people along their historical path, but it can also be a place of despair. Whether America's cities will reverse their now nearly century-long decline depends on whether they can attain the natural, middle level of political identification within the political arrangement that they truly represent.

As Aristotle understood, no nation can survive with political identifications that exist only at the level of the family and the nation. The larger cities of any modern nation are the heart of that nation, just as the cities of the Golden Age were the heart of ancient Greece. But, again, cities are qualitatively, not just quantitatively, different from towns and rural areas. Inherently the home of the most heterogeneous populations in the polity, they are more truly in need of public attention because they are more truly of a public nature than are rural areas, towns, and states. Accordingly, they are entitled to be represented at their appropriate level of political identification not only for their own sake, but also for what their heterogeneity and public nature contribute to the larger political system.

The fact that American cities continue to bear not only the burden of their states' past discrimination but also the burden of a political identification that is different from what it should be hurts the nation now more than ever before. In contrast to how our cities may have fared within a unitary political arrangement, and in contrast to how other countries value their cities, America's divided metropolitan areas are now both estranged from the national government and suffering from an increasingly diluted influence within their own states.

In the American political arrangement, in summary, political discrimination against the city originated in the federal constitutional structure and was exacerbated by the states. As a result, urban representation has been improperly diminished at both the state and federal levels. Ironically, as the American city became more and more of an aggregation of rich diversities in the nation's population, it was the federal system, designed to protect a diversity of political units rather than a diversity of nationalities, that precluded the city from assuming its proper political role.

The Current Choice

If Aristotle's levels of political legitimacy are still the true levels of personal and political identification, the family, as the immediate political unit, and the nation, as the most distant, are far different today from what they were in Aristotle's time. Unaltered, however, are their *positions* in the polity, either in America or anyplace else. Only the village, that intermediate identification with its nearly self-contained yet intimate identity, has been disenfranchised more completely in the United States than it has been in any other nation. Whereas the American polity has maintained the sanctity of the other two levels of identification, it has never sanctified the third, in which 80 percent of the population now lives.

Although originating in the Framers' lack of foresight, the current distortion of political identity that afflicts the American city has been maintained in great part by a misunderstanding on the part of suburban dwellers concerning their true political identity. The suburban dweller has believed, and has been encouraged to believe, in a political existence wholly apart from the city. That belief, of course, has reinforced those arrangements that have permitted the suburb to ignore its obligation to the city. This lack of a sense of political obligation, initially made possible by the Framers's lack of foresight, continues today because of the discriminatory and in some cases unconstitutional strategies perpetuated by the political institution that still improperly supplants the natural intermediate identification of the city—the state.

The short of it is that cities still suffer political discrimination, not only at the hands of their own states, but even more importantly because they lack a direct political relationship to the national government. The absence of such a relationship is rooted, of course, in the constitutional position of the state in the American federal arrangement. But today, cities find it even more difficult to attain what would be their proper relationship to the federal government because of the newly elongated structure of that government and that government's relationship to the private intrusions of the Beltway consultant, the Washington lawyer-lobbyist, and the elections industry on the public domain.

As these new barriers to popular government have altered the private-to-public and legal-to-political balances of the government, they have interfered with the government's ability to deal with just the kinds of nonprivate, nonlegal difficulties that cities more than anyplace else typically suffer. In other words, the national government, newly elongated to stretch out through Washington's ancillary institutions to the private interests that influence governmental affairs, handicaps the American city in its competition for national attention with the suburbs, with the states, and, most importantly, with private, nongovernmental interests.

Aristotle never envisioned this setting of one level of political identification against another. Knowing that each identification, properly, only complemented the others—knowing, in fact, that all identifications were necessary to the survival of each—Aristotle rightly maintained that cooperation among all levels of political identification was necessary for a vital polity. As Aristotle would have foreseen, the American mislocation of its intermediate level of political identification harms more than just that level. The imbalance among the three levels of political identification now threatens the nation as a whole, for it is in the cities that crime, poor housing, drugs, and most of America's other pressing national problems have been most severe.

It will not be easy to realign the formal levels of the American constitutional arrangement with the natural identifications of its citizenry. Our formal constitutional order is substantially what it was at the time of the nation's founding: specifically, it is still federal, not unitary. But as suggested earlier, the United States government in order to rebalance its three levels of political identification may need to recognize the metropolitan areas of the nation in some formal way: for example, by ensuring some form of representation for cities within the national legislature, in much the same way that the Framers ensured representation for the states in the Senate. This proposal, to be sure, involves altering the original contract between the states and the federal government. But such alterations would be appropriate to the natural political identifications of the nation. They would now more correctly represent the true purpose of the Framers with regard to levels of political identification than does the original constitutional arrangement.

Beyond specific issue of the cities, if the United States is to continue to empower two national legislative bodies (the ad-

vanced industrial nations of the world having substantially reduced the powers of their upper houses), then the upper legislative body must no longer be the anachronism that it has become.
The states are not *estates* in the eighteenth- or even seventeenth-
century meaning of that term. Of course, the 20 percent of the
nation's citizens who live outside metropolitan regions must be
guaranteed fair representation as well. But the cities, as the victims of both the Framers' understandable lack of foresight and
the states' less understandable discriminations, deserve the place
in our constitutional arrangement that both Aristotle and the antifederalists (if not the federalists) would give them were they here
today.

If the Civil War was America's deepest political crisis, and if
that war was made more likely by the retention within the Constitution of the concept of state sovereignty that had existed
under the Articles of Confederation, then we would do well to
ponder two historical facts about the states that seceded for a
time: their argument for leaving was based on the most literal
and most contractual understanding of the federal Constitution;
and the ultimate failure of the Confederacy, in great part,
stemmed from its own decentralized nature. It has been said that
the United States government now resembles a kind of confederacy within a world of more modern, better constituted national
governments. In the face of a sanctified 200-year-old constitutional arrangement and of the ironic reinforcement of state jurisdictions following the Civil War, the challenge of achieving
Aristotle's levels of political identifications in the modern American context is perhaps greater than it has been at any time in this
century. But the United States can no longer afford to ignore that
challenge if it is to revitalize American democracy and save
America's cities.

7

America's Political Parties

Party and Government

The least-defined and the least firmly structured institution in any government except the most totalitarian is the political party. Only in totalitarian political systems is the role of the party un-ambivalent. In democratic political systems, the party is a reflection of the political culture and as much a product of all of a free people's wants as a totalitarian party is the single product of what a totalitarian ruler wants it to be. In modern democratic systems, therefore, a political party should take on much of the aggregation of the polity that was assigned to the aristocracy in Aristotle's political order. A party, like Aristotle's aristocracy, must lend cohesion to its polity and at the same time mediate between the citizenry and the government.

The relationship of a political party to its government in a democracy, therefore, encompasses something more than the representation of individual interests before the government. It also includes the collection of public attitudes concerning complex and far-reaching political issues and the melding of such attitudes into constellations of public ideology. Generally, the collective, aggregational task for parties is more important than the task of representing individual interests. Avenues other than those provided by a political party, such as those facilitated by the lawyer-lobbyist in the American political system, are already open to those who wish to make specific, nonmajoritarian demands on the government. To fulfill its obligation properly, then, a political party must have a special relationship to the government. Properly thought of as more of a public institution than a private one, it must be credible with the government and capable of influencing governmental institutions in a way appropriate to the structure of that government.

In view of the need for such credibility with the government, great variations in the forms of political parties have always existed within equally democratic nations. But generally, if a political party has participated in both the election of public officeholders and the governance of the nation in some meaningful way, it is considered to have been performing its role properly.

In the United States, however, an unusually decentralized government and an unusually large and diverse population require that parties, particularly the Democratic Party, undertake an unusual burden. All things being equal, it is appropriate for political parties to mirror the form of the government with which they interact, as well as mirror the political culture. But all things are not equal in America. In the context of the American constitutional order at the close of the twentieth century, American political parties, again at least the Democratic Party, must complement rather than reinforce either the structure of the government or the individualism of the political culture. The Democratic Party particularly must share in the burden of compensating for the nation's newly unbalanced institutional arrangements as well as for the new imbalances between its private and public and its legal and political domains. It must, in short, engage in even more aggregation than it otherwise would.

For example, within the Democratic Party's representative function, whether in the representation of particular interests for which political parties in other countries rarely act, or in the representation of a general perspective upon the public good for which America's parties should do more, the party must now provide a far better political link between the citizenry as a whole and its officeholders. As all of the world's political parties in one way or another provide for a *forming* of the public issues that confront the government, America's parties, and again particularly the Democrats, now have a special obligation to describe the *patterns* in which public issues should, first, be understood by the public and, second, decided by the government.

As noted earlier, there are two very different forms of influence upon the government: the Tocquevilleian form, which carries the individual, usually immediate, demand of a singular political interest to the government; and the majoritarian form, which carries the public will, in a general sense, to the government. In the United States, the nature of the constitutional order has always meant that political parties to some extent, and more so in recent years, define a disproportionate number of political issues in the Tocquevilleian, individual mode. The United States government has become increasingly unprepared to aggregate its public policies, in part because its political parties have not framed our public issues in an aggregational mode.

Implicit in Madison's argument in *The Federalist* is a fear of patterned definitions of political issues. The limited democracy that the federalists defined surely reflected that fear. But Madison's fears alone do not account for the current inability of America's parties, and particularly the Democratic Party, to define public issues in a patterned, aggregational way. Incentives for parties to facilitate specific interest representation and thus reinforce the governmental form that responds best to such representation have grown since Madison's time. But even as America's geography, population, ethnic diversity, and complex postindustrial order have all worked against an understanding of America's political issues in any aggregational, patterned way, the selfishness of those who have prevented parties from assuming their proper role has also contributed significantly to America's party decline.

Not unexpectedly, the price that America pays for its lack of party-led issue aggregation has grown considerably over the last 200 years. Although there have of course been other times when the absence of a comprehensive vision to which a majority could repair has harmed the nation—the period immediately preceding the Civil War being the most notable—America now more than ever pays a heavy price for parties that do not carry a majoritarian political agenda from the people to the government. America's precarious global position and the fact that competing governments in Western Europe and to some degree in Asia aggregate their public policies far more readily than we, reveal the price of our unbalanced parties.

The Rebalancing of America's Parties

If the federalists overwhelmingly preferred to place parties at the periphery of America's public decision making, they did so because they wished specifically to forestall parties from achieving a broad level of cooperation among America's constitutional institutions. It is noteworthy that political parties are never mentioned in the Constitution, either in the seven original Articles or in any of the twenty-six amendments. Today, Madison's admonition against "factions" still influences a political culture that is overly wary of majorities and overly comfortable with what appears to be, though it seldom is, consensus. This sense of comfort must change, not only because political parties are an indispensable organ of modern government, but also because, again, political parties must serve as the principal aggregators of the issues facing a citizenry and its government.

How, then, should the United States resurrect its parties and rebalance the forms of influence that impact on the government? The best answer lies within the prescription for political parties made by the early American who best understood them—Thomas Jefferson. In considerable contrast to James Madison and the federalists, Jefferson insisted that there were two "natural" parties in all political communities. As he put it, "the division between whig and tory is founded in the nature of men."[1] Just as the perilous early condition of our nation responded well to Jefferson's use of his own party when he became president, so too America's present decline enjoins us to recall Jefferson's notion in rebalancing our parties.

In order to rebalance our parties and specifically in order to enhance our parties' impact on the government, we must first question the structure of parties as "bottom-up" organizations. America's parties, like its officeholders, still primarily represent local and statewide interests at the expense of national interests. Apart from the influence of the electoral interests discussed above, the internal structures of the two great American parties, the Republicans and the Democrats, reflect local priorities. If America is to accept the Jeffersonian prescription for its political parties, if it is to place a long-overdue emphasis on the national as opposed to the local good, both national parties to some degree, but particularly the Democratic Party, must be strengthened both structurally and electorally.

It is only fair to acknowledge that, considering its ideological position in the context of the American political argument, the Republican Party's localism and general preference for somewhat less-patterned understandings of national political issues is more appropriate for it than it is for the Democrats. The Republican oscillations between a Burkeian, Eastern corporatism and a more individualistic, Western conservatism have been tumultuous at times but they have rarely prevented the party from making what for it is an appropriate political argument with regard to the balance, for example, of the country's private and public domains. The party of business still largely trusts the private sector to render appropriate productive and distributive judgments for America's citizens and its own localized and decentralized structure does not denigrate that trust.

Particularly in the political contests of recent years, it should be noted that the Republican Party has been successful both in winning presidential elections and in convincing the public of the necessity for restricting the public and expanding the private domain. Accordingly, administrations such as those of Ronald Reagan were successful in redirecting the federal government away from a number of regulative tasks that it had undertaken in the last half-century. Again, however, the Republican Party's belief in a limited role for the government, along with its belief in a more decentralized party, understandably originates in its naturally "tory" position on the division between private and public jurisdictions.

The Democratic Party, in contrast, is nowhere near where it should be in American politics—not only on a large number of substantive questions but, more importantly, on those issues that concern the recent informal restructuring of the government. In the first instance, it is not where it should be with regard to the balance of centrifugal and centripetal forces within its own party structures. Although it has laudably endorsed the participation of all Americans in the general political process as well as in its own processes by opening avenues of participation in party affairs in ways that the Republicans have not, the Democratic Party has largely abandoned its historical positions on the balance of America's private-to-public domains and on the structural integrity of the federal government in the wake of its recent disassembling.

Apart from the abandonment of its traditional private-to-public position, and even apart from its recent acquiescence in the restructuring of the government, two other circumstances also prevent the Democratic Party from being the national party that it should be. The first is the sensitive, important matter of the American South. For all of the amalgamation of American culture that has ostensibly occurred because of television, travel, improved education, and the like, and for all of the 125 years that have now passed since the Civil War, the American South still remains a culturally and politically distinct region of America. The reasons for this distinctiveness, of course, go well beyond the Civil War and the justifiable reaction of the South to what was an unnecessarily harsh and corrupt period of postwar Reconstruction. But had there been no war at all, the strength of the Southern region's identity with its land, its families, its churches, and its unique though often benighted history would still have made it a region apart from the remainder of America.

For a long time after the Civil War, the Southern voter sided overwhelmingly with the Democratic Party, both because of Abraham Lincoln's opposition to secession and because of Reconstruction. More recently, in the wake of the Democratic Party's appropriate commitment to political and economic opportunity for blacks, those who still suffered the effects of their ancestors' bondage, and in the wake of what was surely a false painting of the South as the only situs of racial intolerance in the nation, white Southern voters have largely deserted the Democratic Party, particularly in presidential elections.

The white Southern vote, however, is not a monolithic political unit. Further, from the perspective of the Southerner, a monolithic vote for the presidency, or for any considerable office, is not advantageous either individually or as a resident of this distinct region. If our political parties are to be divided along the old cleavages of race and region in a way that continues to accentuate rather than mute the racial and regional divisions of the country, the country as a whole will surely suffer. Without losing their regional and cultural identity, white Southern voters, particularly moderate thinkers among them, should and will spread their political allegiances more evenly over time. When that happens, Democratic national and state officeholders should be prepared to concur with Jefferson's prescription for a strong national party that speaks to national issues in a comprehensive, patterned way.

But the uniqueness of the South does not account alone for the Democratic Party's inability to perform its proper political role. The Democratic Party's failure to assume its appropriate position on the structure of the government must also be assigned to its congressional officeholders, Northern as well as Southern. Although in control of the House of Representatives since 1954 and of the Senate for almost all of that time, Democratic officeholders have acquiesced in the recent weakening of the government and the corresponding intrusion of the private domain's influence into the government without measurable opposition. Largely because of an inordinate attention to the maintenance of their congressional majorities, Democratic members of Congress have become almost indistinguishable from Republicans in their opposition to party funding of political campaigns and other party-centered improvements that would facilitate majoritarian forms of citizen influence on the government.

Accompanying this silence on matters of form has been silence on the part of all too many Democrats on crucial substantive political issues. Although ostensibly concerned with such matters as the deregulation of the thrift industry, the decline of health and education standards for so many citizens, the low level of environmental enforcement, and similar—what Jefferson would see as natural—Democratic positions, congressional Democrats have participated in the very maladaptive alterations of Congress's informal structures of the government that have led to our government's failure to meet the public's needs. The Republican Party, its constituents and its officeholders, have benefited the most from (1) the extensions of the informal government to the ancillary governmental institutions, (2) the growing centrifugality of the government's own structures, and (3) the increasing influence of the private domain in the government's affairs. The Democratic Party has failed to address any of these alterations in the context of political structure.

The Democratic Party and Government

Where, then, should the Democratic Party stand with regard to the role of the federal government in the solution of a variety of modern political problems? Not surprisingly, the one public issue that perhaps best exemplifies the structural problems besetting the American government today and that the Democratic Party has been negligent in addressing is now, if belatedly, coming before the American people. That issue centers around the structure of the government itself, or what many call the "gridlock" of the federal government. Without question, the increases in the public debt, the inability of the government to develop an effective industrial policy, the still ineffective protections of the environment, and a variety of other governmental incapacities now fairly reflect a government that has become a collection of institutions that are increasingly fragmented and increasingly incapable of providing for the nation's well-being.

Because the structural difficulties of the American political system have resulted from an excess of centrifugal institutional and extra-institutional forces, and because these structural difficulties are accentuated by, among other things, a lack of coordination between the government's executive and legislative branches, two very different remedies suggest themselves. The choice between these remedies provides an excellent example of the kinds of political preference that Jefferson's prescriptions for political parties would suggest today.

When two institutions—or two individuals, for that matter—do not cooperate well, two solutions are always available. The first is to improve the level of cooperation between the institutions by ameliorating their differences and encouraging their mutual regard for a common goal. This remedy is, in a manner of speaking, a "horizontal" solution, in that it respects and maintains a rough parity between the two institutions. The other, conceptually "vertical," remedy is to attempt to assure progress toward the common goal by making one entity clearly superior to the other in the working out of the current difficulty. This remedy does not assume, and surely does not respect, the equality of the two entities.

In creating the institutional structures of the federal government, the Framers, of course, provided for the separation of federal powers by means of checks and balances between those powers. Checks and balances are distinct concepts, each of which makes a separate contribution to America's political structure. *Checks* are best defined as those cautionary safeguards that one branch of the government enforces upon the other in order to forestall the dominance of a single branch. The presidential veto of congressional action, the congressional overrides of such vetoes, the advice and consent that the Senate gives on the principal executive appointments, and the right of Congress to prescribe for the judicial jurisdiction are all explicit checks within the American constitutional order.

The *balances* of the Constitution, on the other hand, are both more subtle and less explicit than its checks. Growing out of the Framers' desire to have the three branches of the government be roughly equal in power, the balances of the government do nothing more and nothing less than ensure that the historical swings of legislative to presidential ascendance that have occurred throughout American history are both moderate and temporary. Without question, the Framers' idea of balances in the Constitution prevents the installation of permanent imbalances between Congress and the presidency in the American constitutional order.

Within this understanding of the nature of constitutional checks and balances, the issue of constitutional "gridlock" has generated two very different political solutions. Not surprisingly, those solutions reflect the natural positions of the two American parties, one prescribing for an essentially "vertical" remedy, and the other prescribing for an essentially "horizontal" remedy. The Republican solution, drawn from the precedent of several state governments, is that the president of the United States be permitted to ease governmental gridlock by exercising a "line item" veto. Armed with this power, which would require constitutional amendment (although some Republicans argue that it does not), the president could selectively approve or disapprove of each separate provision within any bill passed by Congress, rather than either wholly accept or wholly decline a piece of legislation. Because this "vertical" solution would considerably imbalance the relative powers of Congress and the president in favor of the latter, it arguably comes close to, if it does not actually constitute, a fundamental violation of the prescription for balances that the Framers provided. In a historical context, it is not far distant from a Stuart vision of a strong executive, a weak legislature, and a government of limited public jurisdiction.

The competing solution to governmental gridlock, appropriately, is the one that addresses the checks rather than the balances of the Constitutional order. Under this horizontal remedy, which would move our political system ever so slightly closer to that of the European parliamentary systems, members of the legislature could serve as cabinet and subcabinet officers in the executive branch, representatives' term of office would be extended from the current two to four years, and state governments would be mandated to provide for party-line voting—an option that some states already have whereby each party's candidates for the offices of the presidency, the Senate (if applicable), and the House of Representatives be available on the same voting lever. Without question, such measures would enhance the level of cooperation between the legislative and executive branches at a time of growing discord between those branches, without minimizing the role of the federal legislature.

To return to the matter of the Democratic Party and its negligence in addressing these issues, we should note the current political status of the two alternative methods of resolving America's "gridlock." Whereas the current president of the United States, a Republican, and the most recent past president of the United States, also a Republican, now regularly advocate the line-item veto, the Jefferson-founded Democratic Party, which according to the Jeffersonian notion should be equally vigorous in support of the historic role of the democratic legislature and the importance of interbranch, party-led institutional cooperation in the government, has been virtually silent on this issue. A few prominent Democratic members of Congress, such as Senator Edward M. Kennedy of Massachusetts, have even endorsed the line-item veto.

The central reason for the Democrat's silence on the issue of the line-item veto and, more generally, the issue of the constitutional gridlock, is, unfortunately, that Democratic officeholders in Congress, in spite of a clear threat to their constitutional prerogative on legislation, prefer the prerogatives of their linkages with their constituents. Considering the appropriate position of the Democratic Party in American politics, as well as the history of the party and the history of the debate between the federalists and the antifederalists, the congressional Democratic Party's betrayal of what would and should be its natural position on the issue of governmental gridlock is inexcusable.

Recall that Thomas Jefferson not only was the first to understand political parties in the new American democracy but was also the first to use the party in a politically meaningful way. Recall, too, that it was Democrat Andrew Jackson who first cultivated the politics of popular democracy, and it was Democrat Woodrow Wilson whose progressivism fostered passage of the income tax, the direct election of senators, the enfranchisement of women, the creation of the Federal Reserve Board, and a variety of legislative measures that dealt with the working conditions of the American laborer. Finally, it was Democrat Franklin Roosevelt's New Deal that shaped the government's role vis-à-vis the private domain as it had never been shaped before. The natural position of the Democratic Party must continue to be, as it has been at its best in the past, one of a revitalization, not a dismemberment, of the government. Only with that form of Democratic input can the government fulfill its public obligation.

The American political party, more so than the parties of other democratic nations, will no doubt continue to be as vaguely defined in the American political arrangement as it has always been. But the Democratic Party, as it has not yet done, must repair to its historical role and bring before the American people the issues of the government's need to reconstitute itself and the government's need to rebalance America's private domain with an effective public domain. In the final analysis, the mark of any political system that purports to be democratic is not whether there is more than one political party in the system. In the final analysis, democracy is measured by the range of discussion that the political system at large permits. Conceivably, a nation with only one party may allow more wide-ranging discussions of public issues than does the United States, which has, at least nominally, two political parties. The range of the political discussion in America today is narrower than it has been at any time in the last half-century. And, sadly, the Democratic Party, during the past twenty years of our country's decline, has simply failed to engender even the most cursory examination of the deeper reasons for that decline.

The long-term well-being of the Democratic Party, and with it the long term well-being of our country, require that the Party do in our time nothing more and certainly nothing less than what it did during America's other times of trial. The Democratic Party must encourage, not discourage, the broadest possible discussion of America's fundamental, structurally based political difficulties. Eventually, it must adopt a position on these structural difficulties that is consistent with its Jeffersonian, democratic heritage.

Note

1. Dumas Malone, *The Sage of Monticello*. Boston: Little, Brown, 1981, p. 203.

8

Congress

Forms of Representation

Like Solon of Athens, the senators of Rome, and the early parliamentarians of England, the members of the United States Congress are a part of history's democratic thread. England bequeathed our nation a democratic tradition that left little question of what Americans would expect of their legislature. Only a fully representative body would do, for in terms of institutions a representative legislature is the benchmark of a democratic government.

The greatest compromise within the Constitutional Convention was that forged over the issue of representation in Congress. In opposing camps were the large and small states, each group seeking to advance its own interests and the interests of its expectantly democratic citizens at the same time. A new Republic would not have emerged from the convention if what appeared to each to be fair representation had not been arranged. The resulting Connecticut Compromise was not easily arrived at, but it was well in keeping with what democracy, as understood at the time, called for. There would be not one but two houses, one for the states and one for the people, the states' chamber serving as a check on the popular assembly. The upper body, in turn, would be checked by the election of its members from each statehouse and not from each state's people. The antifederalists did not trust the Senate, expecting it to be the home of an untitled aristocracy. The federalists did not trust the House, in which a popular majority might rise up to dominate the nation, as had happened in several states.

But the Connecticut Compromise was about far more than the conflict between large and small states: it was about how the nation would shape its democracy. As a result of the compromise, there would be a division within a division in the government—a cleavage beyond the separation of powers. Was American democracy so secure that it could divide its government twice over? Or was it so insecure that it could do nothing else?

Over the years, the bifurcated legislature checked itself and its people just as the antifederalists feared that it would. Although there have been shifts in prestige and power between the House and Senate, neither chamber, nor Congress as a whole, has ever managed majoritarianism. When the popular election of Senators began in 1913, the distinction between the chambers became little more than a division. That division remains today for, unlike in Europe where governments have largely excused their upper houses as they have excused their estates, the Senate has precisely the power that it was given at the convention.

It is within the legislative houses, rather than between them, that significant changes in Congress have occurred. Burdened, to be sure, with more complex tasks in our time, Congress has built a vastly more complex structure for itself. Staffs have grown, calendars have lengthened, and committees have become more fragmented as they have become more independent of their houses. Those committees, in turn, have spawned subcommittees, working groups, and informal subunits of even smaller vision. The antifederalists' worry over the paucity of representatives, ironically, is more appropriate for the Senate today. As the Senate's substructures narrow its vision, its hundred legislators may be stretched too thinly to master either the specifics of necessary legislation or the larger vision of public good. The Senate may now be even less democratic than the federalists intended.

The current generation of congressional members has argued that circumstances have forced them to make these changes. Yet, even with the jet airplane and the coming of new means of communication between the represented and the representer, that argument is unconvincing. In its all-too-permanent bicameral division, the congressional balance between the majoritarian demands for popular legislation and the antimajoritarian checks that protected private and legal prerogatives is more precarious now than ever before. How the delicate preconstitutional balance of individual-to-majoritarian democracy has been affected is a result, directly, of what the members have added to Congress.

The most notable addition to Congress has been an immense staff. The significance of this addition lies not only in its size but also in the nature of what Congress's 23,000 staff members do. Properly speaking, the people who work for the members of Congress are no longer congressional staff members. Rather, as they are hired by, and loyal to, and thus serve individual members alone, they are apart from the body, apart from the core of Congress. The committees, too, have increasingly grown apart from the core of Congress. They are the province of their chairs, still selected informally by seniority, in spite of meager attempts at party caucus authority. These committee chairs, too, have their staffs, hired only by them and loyal only to them. Even the ranking minority members obtain similar patterns of staff allegiance. Congress's structure, beyond its constitutional division, has thus continued to fragment, and as a result the members are more unto themselves and their constituents, and less to the body as a whole, than they have ever been before.

The Congressional Environment

What has gone on within Congress, to be sure, has had a great deal to do with what has gone on outside it. But if times have changed, so has the nature of those who regularly deal with Congress. America's private interests, in encouraging the increasingly disparate, legalistic, and private altering of the American constitutional order generally, have made Congress their principal target.

A rebalancing of Congress would be difficult enough if the causes of its imbalances were solely internal. Adding to that difficulty, however, is the fact that the recapturing of congressional authority will require confronting each of the agents of Congress's outside interests. The consultants of the Beltway, the avenues of influence of the Washington lawyer-lobbyists, and the reelection-assuring and thus seemingly indispensable elections industry all have a stake in keeping Congress just as it has recently become. The devolutions of the country's politics into private hands has been far more damaging to Congress than, say, the involvement of congressional members in personal scandals. Structurally rebalancing Congress will be difficult because the work of Congress, or the work that Congress was enjoined to do by the Constitution, is now less and less done by Congress. The preparation of legislation, the channeling of legislation through the steps of congressional acceptance, and the protection of the legislator throughout the process are increasingly performed by the other Washington institutions that have informally become a part of the government. The American Congress now surely violates Edmund Burke's admonition that a legislator should bring only "his unbiased opinion, his mature judgment [and] his enlightened conscience" to the national legislature.[1]

What has gone on in Congress is nothing less than a partial surrender of congressional sovereignty. To the degree that the institutions of the Beltway, the Washington lawyer-lobbyist, and the elections industry have become part of the government, or have extended the government's structure to include their own institutions, Congress has become less central to the government. We should not forget that Congress's own balances and thus its centrality to the government involve more than structural matters. They also involve the balancing of the competing claims of the private and public domains, as well as the claims of the individual and majoritarian appeals to the government. Although the Framers insisted on protections for the private domain, the present calamity is that Congress, like the government itself, is increasingly becoming a private body.

To legislate for the public good is what a democratic legislature must do. Accordingly, a democratic legislature must institute a set of internal procedures that facilitate such legislation. But the nature of the legislative product is equally the result of the character of the legislative institution. A reconciliation of legislative requests is necessary in the American Congress, as it is with any legislature, but that reconciliation cannot be achieved within a Congress that is losing its identity amid a welter of private interests whose claims alone Congress is enjoined to make into public policy.

The American Congress's democratic role, then, has been impaired by a fundamental misadjustment of its relationship to both the remainder of the government and the people. And those impairments have come in two ways, not just one, for although the thread of democracy requires a proximity of the legislature to both its people and to whatever else makes up the government, that proximity can be too close with regard to individual contact and too distant with regard to contact with the general will of the people. More importantly, that proximity can be of such a nature that the institution loses its integrity in an incestuous proximity to the individual, private form of external influence.

Reforming Congress

Any redressing of Congress's recent alterations will require an extension of its jurisdictional boundary in both directions. Looking inward, the body must restore its structural integrity through the actions of its leadership, its parties, and its party caucuses as well as through a revival of the sometimes necessarily cloistered forum for the discussion of all public issues. Looking outward, the body must regain distance not simply from those expectant public pressures that bring influence to legislatures on various issues but also from the overwhelming private, individual influences that are intrusive to the degree that they obscure the jurisdictional boundaries of the institution itself.

Again, a legislative body does not represent the legislative ideal simply by summing the totality of all representations to it by private, singular interests. A legislative body, and the public interest that it ultimately represents, requires a quality of attention to the legislative enterprise that is, in some way, divorced from and yet aggregative of all interests. As Edmund Burke and others understood, not only must the legislator be protected from a plethora of direct and specific influences, particularly at the moment of legislation, but the legislative body itself must provide the shield that offers that protection. In recent years, individualistic influences have vastly outweighed majoritarian influences in the United States Congress precisely because of the inability of Congress to provide that shield. American democracy has suffered accordingly as a result of this inability.

A Representative Issue

It is not coincidental that the structural imbalances of America's national legislature have affected its work in yet another way. Recently, much controversy has arisen with regard to the remuneration of legislators. This issue, though of some importance in and of itself, is more significant for what it says about the nature of Congress and the government as a whole. Proponents of congressional pay raises argue, correctly, that metropolitan Washington has become an inordinately expensive place to live. Maintenance of a residence in or around the city, along with the seemingly obligatory maintenance of a residence in the district or state that the member represents, surely imposes a double burden on the congressional salary.

Yet, even though the salary of the congressional member must allow for two homesites and must also be sufficient to encourage America's ablest citizens to serve in Congress, a democratic nation must never allow the standard of reward for its legislative officeholders, or for any other national governmental officers, to become a Capital rather than a national standard. The legitimacy of a legislature, in the sense that it is still perceived as being a representative body of a democratic people, is more important than any legislative product of that body. It is certainly more important than the legislator's ability to provide for more than a commodious standard of living during his or her congressional service.

Beyond legitimacy, there is another, more important, reason why a Capital standard of congressional salary must never be used. An issue that must be addressed is congressional acceptance or rejection of the circumstances that have made Washington, D.C., the expensive place that it is. It is not, and it never has been, the remuneration of legislators, bureaucrats, the military, or other government employees that has made Washington's standard of living so much higher than it is in virtually any part of the country. The high cost of a Washington residence is largely the result of two extraordinary phenomena, neither of which is supportive of high salaries for the congressional member. The first is the explosive growth of the newly governmental, ancillary institutions. The high cost of the "services" that ancillary institutions such as the Beltway consultant, the Washington lawyer-lobbyist, and the elections industry provide have had much to do with making the city more expensive than it needs to be. The second cause of the high cost of living in Washington is the condition of much of the city, a condition that has come about in great part because of the failure of the government, and particularly the constitutionally mandated Congress, to address the tragedy of Washington's nongovernmental citizens.

Thus, although a reasonably generous remuneration for member of Congress is supportable on several grounds, the best response to those who argue for significant increases in remuneration is that it is the unelected, ancillary officers of America's government that are vastly overpaid and who should have their usefulness to the government, and thus their salaries, diminished. These individuals' high salaries—a result, incidentally, of the ready availability of those resources by which the unelected influence Congress—have placed the congressional member at a disadvantage in competing for available housing and services, just as these individuals' influence in Washington has placed the congressional member at a disadvantage in his or her legislative role. The largesse of America's ancillary government has led directly to the bidding up of housing prices in metropolitan Washington's preferred neighborhoods to the point where Washington's bedrooms have become outrageously expensive, just as the newly institutionalized position of Washington's ancillary officeholders has led directly to the bidding up of the price of the general public's access to its government.

But beyond the bidding up of Washington's private residences by the government's ancillary officers, the unavailability of safe housing near the Capitol and other government buildings affects the price of all Washington's housing. Americans know what has happened to the city of Washington in recent years: the infliction of drugs upon the citizenry; the infliction of a drug-attendant level of crime upon the citizenry; the infliction of homelessness, unemployment, and fear and malaise among the city's population is certainly unmatched anywhere else in a capital city in the developed world. These conditions, naturally, restrict the area in which a member of Congress, with or without a family, would wish to live. The cost of homes in those more distant living areas where congressional members do live has risen accordingly.

To a degree, of course, the government's, and particularly Congress's, attention to the clients of the ancillary Washington institutions instead of the residents of Washington is simply a matter of the relative resources of the two groups. But differences in the government's attention to one problem over another have resulted in greater part from the imbalances in the kinds of access to the national government that have occurred in recent years. Those imbalances, as we have seen, have meant that single-interest representation has excluded less well-defined interests from political consideration. As the political interests of Washington's nongovernmental citizens are certainly more complex than any question of trade protection, tax relief, or the like, the imbalance of governmental attention away from the former concerns is only further guaranteed.

In sum, it is not much of a stretch to say that the current condition of the city of Washington is simply a somewhat exaggerated microcosm of the larger country's condition. As the discrete, private interest is increasingly all that survives the government's structural revisions, this condition can be remedied only by a return to the forms of government that permit attention to what are the nation's truly public issues. The public interest, which has recently become so ill-defined and so residual to what is done in the Washington government, needs to find a renewed, majoritarian access to its government and particularly to Congress that will be signaled by better treatment of Washington's own citizens to their government.

In the last analysis, then, the matter of congressional salary is not so much a matter of the remuneration itself as it is of the current representative reality of the government. That reality now includes a placement of the public officeholder in a disadvantaged financial position, as well as in a position of political dependency on others in the way he or she conducts the public's business. A commitment on the part of Congress to resume its fully public character, to regenerate its own sources of expertise under the general authority of the congressional leadership, and to rebalance access to its own halls must be made if Congress is to regain its democratic role in the American political system.

The Irony of Congressional Service

Beyond the now-subordinate position of so many of Congress's members with respect to the holders of the government's ancillary positions and the private interests that lie behind them, one further difficulty besets Congress. Although most of the Framers were comfortable in their financial circumstances, they were not all wealthy men, and they did not intend that democratic representation in the government should be restricted to those of considerable means. This is precisely what has happened, however. In great part because of the changed character of the government and of Congress's relationship to its ancillary institutions, only the wealthy can now serve there. Within the Senate particularly, but even increasingly within what was designed as the popular chamber, fewer and fewer citizens of less than considerable means have been able to run for office in recent years. This fact speaks to the increasingly undemocratic character of Congress almost as much as do the structural changes that have taken place in it. These two realities, of course, are strongly related.

An additional threat to democracy results from the juxtaposition of an issue such as that of remuneration with the other issues that now surround Congress. In recent years retired or (in rare cases) defeated members of Congress have increasingly tended to remain in Washington after their congressional service because of the prospects for profitable enterprise that have become available to them there. Overwhelmingly, members have chosen to repair specifically to the ancillary institutions of the government, that is to those institutions that have recently so corrupted the legislature. In Washington, the recently corrupted now more than ever find it to their advantage to join the corrupters.

Partly, of course, so many former members of Congress have joined the ancillary government because the remuneration there is so generous. But they also have joined the ancillary government because they suspect, quite rightly, that the ancillary positions have now become the places where the true power of Washington lies. As a former congressional member is more valuable to those interests that hire him or her for access to existing members, the former member's postcongressional service cumulatively adds to the distortion of Washington's government. It also cumulatively adds to the extension of the governmental structure and further devolves the democratic nature of Congress into the ancillary institutions that foster the extension. As former congressional members become lobbyists, the private-to-public delineation of the government becomes more and more imbalanced, and the sitting congressional member is increasingly reminded that the new arrangement of the Washington government places its power in the hands of people who influence representatives, rather than those who are the people's representatives. The thread of democracy grows thinner as those who abandon democracy's principal institutions increasingly, if unwittingly, abandon democracy itself.

Throughout history, one of the most certain signals of political decline in any polity has been the simultaneous governmental and financial isolation of a government's institutions from the remainder of its citizenry. History records that the decline of public institutions, in one form or another, is invariably marked by a corruption not so much of individuals but of the public purpose of the government itself. Personal corruptions have always been more likely to be the result, not the cause, of the corruption of the government's larger, public purpose.

In a democratic government, particularly one that is as structurally dispersed as is the United States government, the path of decline is clear. When the most fundamental structures of our government, and especially those structures that are so necessary to democracy as the form of representation in the legislature, are such that the character of the legislature itself is altered, the condition signals a dangerous corruption of democracy.

In a democracy, public legislation must not only reflect something more than the sum of private interests seeking to influence their government: public legislation must aggregate legislative initiatives in a way that forestalls narrow and singular representation as the sole structure for doing the public's business. The bedrock guarantee against such perversion comes from maintaining the public nature of the representative, legislative institutions against the demands of singular, private interests. Only then are the structural balances within the legislative institutions maintained and the public good attended to.

For now, the access that individual interests have to the United States Congress and to the rest of the government, facilitated largely by the Washington Beltway consultant, the Washington lawyer-lobbyist, and the member-protecting elections industry, is receptive neither to the underrepresented interest of the nation as a whole or even to the condition of the city in which it resides. As it has been Congress that has been more responsible for the unbalancing of the government than any other governmental institution, so it is Congress that must, first, rebalance its own structures and, second, assist in the rebalancing of the entire government in a way that restores America's democracy.

Note

1. Peter J. Stanlis, ed., *Edmund Burke: Selected Writings and Speeches.* Chicago: Regency Gateway, 1963, p. 187.

9

The Chief Executive

The President and Congress

In the 1830s, Alexis de Tocqueville forecast that the principal price for America's democracy would be the mediocrity of its leaders. He was right. Over lengthy periods of American history (most frequently when the country without admitting it wished not to face an unpleasant difficulty), second-rate and even misguided leaders have served as the nation's chief executives. The penalty for placing such figures in the presidency, as in the period before the Civil War, was often substantial. Today, the price is higher still.

What most concerned Tocqueville, as a matter of politics, was the nineteenth century's evolving choice between aristocratic and democratic forms of government. For Tocqueville, accounting for what was gained and lost by the slow surrender of an aristocracy to history was far more important than what the surrender to executive mediocrity ought to mean for Americans. No remedy for executive mediocrity was provided by Tocqueville but, from today's perspective, no remedy can include anything less than a democratically elected executive within a democratic government. There must be changes, well within the democratic tradition, in both how we select our presidents and how our presidents fulfill the duties of their office.

In seeking to separate the people from their executives, the Framers mandated that the Electoral College intercede between the citizenry and the ultimate selection of a president. Although the Electoral College has been controversial from its inception, the notion of indirectness in the selection of a president is as sound today as it was 200 years ago. The difference is that today, indirectness should come before a final selection by the people, not afterward. It is the political party that should act as the electoral intermediary by better providing the citizenry with a choice of leaders. After the nominating processes of the two major parties has been completed, the final selection should rightfully belong to the people. If the parties perform their function well, the citizenry can then select between alternatives who are neither mediocre nor unrepresentative.

If America's political parties are to offer the best of possible leadership, they must first perceive their larger political task as encompassing more than a selection of two competitors on the basis of personal character, capability, and the like. The justification for the role of the political party as an electoral intermediary at the level of the presidency rests on the party's ability to aggregate those components of the population that potentially support a candidacy and a program. Presidential selection and presidential governance cannot be divorced. A full pattern of governance must be consented to, at least by some majority aggregation of the citizenry. Only the candidate who achieves the highest aggregation can be recognized as deserving the mandate to govern.

The filter of a prior indirectness, the aggregation of the potentially majoritarian governing position within a party's nominating process, thus enhances democracy. It both maintains a key balance of democracy by permitting the full participation of the citizenry in the selection of the president and facilitates an elected president's public purpose once in office. In these ways, a president's leadership obligation can include a reinforcement of the democratic standard as it facilitates the governing of the nation.

In the American political system, in contrast to the parliamentary systems of Europe, it is not obvious that the current party process of selection improves the ability to govern. Whereas European parliamentary leaders are also chosen by indirection, campaigning only in unusually safe electoral districts and elected later by the victorious legislative party that he or she leads, the American presidential candidate campaigns throughout the nation. Unlike the parliamentary leader, the elected American president is therefore unprotected from even the most particular of political claims. As a result of this lack of protection, any sitting American president must spend a great deal of energy in the mere preservation of the integrity of the presidential office in order to govern effectively. Again, such protection does not flow naturally from a political system that is based on the separation of the executive and the legislative powers and upon an indirectness of election that is mediated not by parties but by the Electoral College.

If protection of the president from the immediate influence of private constituencies is therefore more necessary here than it is, say, in a European parliamentary system, how best can it be accomplished? Although the president of the entire citizenry, an American chief executive does best when not serving as a representative of all of the people's groupings. Indeed, the president, unlike the congressional member, should not be considered as a representative of the people at all. A president's governance should embody the party's and some portion of the nation's preferences, but the governance of the president, like the selection of the president, must originate at a place that is outside both party and citizenry.

To govern best, in other words, the president should be at one remove from the citizenry—at one remove from the intrusions of individual interests that have recently changed the American government. Specifically, the president must be the public official farthest from the Beltway, farthest from the lawyer-lobbyist, and farthest from those who would control elections and reelections. In this sense, the president must be the most public of national officeholders, the most immune to the private interest. Of course, the American government, as designed by the Framers, is purposefully open to a variety of influences. But as those influences have outbalanced the public interest and as they have intruded particularly on the United States Congress, a president today must be more the aggregator of the public will than ever before.

Moreover, as individual interests have encouraged the government to spawn the ancillary structures that are increasingly facilitative to outside interests, private, legalistic access to the government and particularly to Congress has impeded the natural process of policy aggregation. As Congress has increasingly come under the influence of the Tocquevillean form of access, the president now stands increasingly alone as the repository of the aggregated public interest. For these reasons, too, the president must not be merely a public representative. The president must be the official farthest away not only from the elongations of the increasingly private government, but also from the influences, often congressionally invited, that so often retard the public interest.

The Presidential Method

In order to fulfill the office's modern obligations, an American president today must remember an essential truth about the government: the Tocquevilleian form of access to the United States government winnows a great deal of the public interest from each legislative initiative. By the time Congress passes a law, the public issue involved has been subjected to pressures that, in their further honing, have left only the least controversial resolutions of a public difficulty within the legislation. The residuum of public necessity that lies outside each legislative initiative by the time it reaches the president, therefore, is considerable. Although the president is obligated to cooperate with Congress, the president has an equal obligation not to collaborate, or, better, not to *collude* with Congress in ratifying the political process that has just narrowed the response to a public need. In being the most public of national officeholders, the president must actively restore the residual public interest in what is now such privately dominated legislation.

Although not a representative, therefore, any American president must have equal standing with Congress in the matter of legislation. But the president must engage the executive branch in a way that is functionally complementary to, not similar to, that of Congress. A president cannot mimic Congress, for the separated powers of the Constitution were not designed by the Framers merely as a separation of substantive jurisdictions. They were designed as a separation of perspectives, a separation that bespeaks a qualitative differentiation in the forms in which each branch defines the public interest. It is not only because the president is elected by all of the people, as no other federal officeholder is, but also because Congress is necessarily a representative institution, with direct and immediate responsibility to the citizenry, that the presidency must fulfill a complementary political function.

The President and the Party

It is apparent, then, that American presidents must do more in the nation's third century than rise above mediocrity. They will soon need to engage in a vigorous attempt at redressing the institutional imbalances of the government by reversing the structurally centrifugal trends that have afflicted the government over the past quarter-century. To restore structural coherence to the American government—even though Congress must retain the principal obligation to rebalance its own centrifugal and centripetal structures—the president can actively encourage change in Congress's way of doing its own business. To do so, the president must understand certain fundamental differences between the American presidential system and the European parliamentary systems.

It is commonly thought that the principal difference between the European parliamentary system and the American presidential system is the combination of the legislative and executive powers in Europe as opposed to the separation of those powers here. This is not true. Though the difference between a government of fusion or fission is important, the most significant difference between the European parliamentary and the American presidential systems has to do with the relationship of the entire government to the citizenry, not the relationship of the parts of the government to each other.

Where the two systems diverge most fundamentally is in the institutionalization of the governing process after the electoral period is over. In parliamentary systems, the prime minister governs as the leader of the party in government and not as a direct representative of the people. Thus it is the party-protected chief, not the individual legislator in government, that in the typical European arrangement is fully at one remove from the people. In the United States, the president, all things equal, is less removed from the people because of the national election of the office. But an elected president can achieve much of the distance available to a parliamentary prime minister from a form of insulation that is already provided in the constitutional framework. Because the presidential term of office is a fixed one, a president, barring serious wrongdoing, will serve a minimum of four years. Time is a fair substitute for space in this regard. Distance from the immediacy of parliamentary no-confidence threats and the vicissitudes of politics that prompt them is something of real executive value in a presidential system.

The president's electoral insularity, as well as the president's constitutional insularity from Congress, therefore, provide an opportunity for each president to embark on a procedural bargain with Congress—a bargain that should help to restore the structural integrity of the American political system. To begin, if Congress will not do so on its own, the president, with as much assistance from sympathetic members of Congress regardless of party as possible, should encourage Congress to finance its elections exclusively with public funds. Further, the president should propose that funding be placed exclusively under the control of the congressional party leadership, not of individual congressional members. Clearly, such active presidential encouragement for an increase in party involvement with congressional candidates would not threaten the balance of power between Congress and the president. Indeed, the success of such one-time involvement would mean that each house of Congress would be more cohesively administered by its party leadership and, thus, stronger vis-à-vis the president than it currently is.

Presidential involvement in this type of reform of Congress, furthermore, would leave congressional members far less beholden to the interests of districts or states and more receptive to long-term, comprehensive perspectives on the public good. Bargaining between the president and Congress could proceed at an enhanced level of concern over difficult public issues, no matter which institution initiates such bargaining. When one or both of the houses of Congress is controlled by the president's party, that party, under the influence of its congressional leadership, could bargain freely with the president with less fear of constituent reprisal. But even when one or both houses are controlled by the non-presidential party, bargaining with that party's leadership could be focused far more on the public interest than it presently is.

Some members of Congress have already opposed and will continue to oppose public, party-controlled funding for their campaigns. But a president who has recently won office is in the best position possible to bring the issue to the citizenry and Congress in a dramatic manner. Members of Congress have, at least publicly, decried the cost of their campaigns. They have also decried the need for almost perpetual fund-raising, and many have recognized that they are now unusually constrained in their wish to do the public good by the private interests that fund their campaigns.

Campaign funding reform would go far toward making Congress less vulnerable to the immediate and individual interests that regularly haunt it, but campaign reform cannot come wholly from within Congress. It must come in great part from a president, or from joint, even preelection, understandings between a president and at least the congressional leadership. A presidential offer of greater autonomy for congressional members, made by a president who is elected by all of the people, would be a powerful political initiative. A president, in line with the notion of the separation of powers that the Framers designed, may better encourage congressional funding reform and structural reform in Congress than may the members themselves.

The Presidential Campaign

Unfortunately, any presidential impetus for campaign funding in Congress and structural reform in the government as a whole would be impeded by the current nature of the American presidential campaign. Any sitting president or aspiring presidential candidate faces an ordeal of election or reelection today that is unmatched anywhere in the world. The travail of the presidential selection process, with its ever-increasing necessity for direct and lengthy interaction with the large and diverse American citizenry, has surely discouraged many capable citizens from seeking the nation's highest public position. Also, even the most public-spirited of American citizens have grown weary of the nation's long and tiresome presidential campaigns. These kinds of campaigns cannot continue.

Even though American presidential campaigns necessarily can never be as brief or as focused as are the party-dominated campaigns of Europe, measures can be taken to improve the process of presidential selection in order to forestall the threat of mediocrity and encourage America's best citizens to run for the presidency. Whatever is done to improve the presidential selection process must complement what is done to improve the congressional one for, apart from restrictions on the expense and length of presidential campaigns, the quality of congressional campaigns must also be improved.

First, the national political parties, in cooperation with each other and in cooperation with their state parties, must both limit the number of presidential primaries and condense the time period in which the entire presidential campaign is allowed to run. Because recent Supreme Court rulings have strengthened the authority of national parties over state parties, shortening the length of the presidential campaign is possible as well as desirable.

By restricting the number of primaries and increasing the number of party caucuses, the parties may also encourage a more articulate rendering of candidate positions on far-reaching public issues than is allowed by the present multiplicity of essentially localized presidential campaigns. At a minimum, restructuring the presidential primaries can ensure the more effective involvement of party figures in the nominating process and reclaim the interest of the American people at that crucial time. Under the current primary format, there is far less meaningful participation than desirable.

It should be clear that as America's congressional campaigns have tended to address only the narrowest and the most local of political issues, America's presidential campaigns must address the most pressing issues facing the country. The presidential contest must be the most educational of campaigns, and must stimulate the people's willingness to make necessary sacrifices. Along with furthering the electoral cases of both candidates, the presidential campaign, far more than any other, should alert the citizenry to the difficulties that lie ahead.

In sum, the essentially nonrepresentative nature of the presidential office, along with the indirectness of governance that the office requires, must no longer be compromised by the format of the presidential campaign. That campaign must be run as far more of a party function than recent presidential campaigns have been. The benefits that European parliamentary systems derive from their separation from the direct and frequent influence of private interests originate in the party-oriented nature of their elections. This separation also results in the highest level of protection that a party can afford once the prime minister is in office. Neither the United States nor any other democratic nation can be governed without the contribution of that public aggregation that comes through political parties or the protection from immediate political clamor that parties give to the officeholder. And this observation is nowhere more valid than it is in the case of the American presidency.

Amid what have been recent "reforms" of the American electoral process, many of which were counterproductive, the cardinal consideration for the revitalization of the presidential electoral procedure must now be that no "reform" should further impede the president from the task of public governance. What

Tocqueville foresaw for this nation with regard to the weakness of executive leadership may have been inevitable in the early years of the Republic. The balance of the experienced and stable leadership that an aristocracy as opposed to a democracy might have offered America at that time no doubt encouraged Tocqueville to adjudge the two designs as more or less even. But we are an older and, hopefully, more mature nation now.

The American government is certainly in a position of far greater public responsibility, both with respect to its own citizens and to the world at large, than it has ever been. Whether we are a more democratic nation, however, is not at all clear. Our pre-constitutional imbalances have permitted a private, unlanded aristocracy to further a de-democratization process in America. If the United States is to continue to be a champion of democracy in the world, this process of de-democratization must be reversed.

It is consistent both with the principles of democracy and with the letter and the spirit of the Framers' Constitution to provide for effective executive leadership. Moreover, although the thread of democracy runs through the legislature, the American presidency—the modern analog to the kings of days gone by, including, we must admit, the Stuarts—may be the last guarantor of an effective, democratic government. Occupants of the presidential office must now prepare themselves to make their full contribution to the rebalancing of America's governmental institutions.

10

A New World

America's Private Leadership

The United States was born a small and vulnerable nation just over 200 years ago. Its birthing was prolonged, the capital being occupied one last time by the mother country nearly forty years after independence. Since then, we have done better. The United States now owns a rightful place on the roll of history's great nations.

But America now finds itself in a period of at least relative decline. Our influence has certainly waned economically, if not politically, in the last twenty-five years vis-à-vis the European and Asian nations. Our relationship with the world, although surely enhanced by the passing of communism from the world stage and hardly subordinate as in the early nineteenth century when our citizens were impressed and our ships plundered by pirates, is marked by more economic vulnerability than it has been at any time in recent memory.

Throughout history, each period of global leadership has differed from the one before it. Certainly, America's form of global leadership was different from those of preceding times. Our nation, even more than Great Britain, achieved its dominance with the assistance of its overwhelmingly private economic institutions. Our global dominance, unlike any other in history, was therefore not principally that of a government. America chose to cast its private institutions onto the world, usually with only subtle reinforcement from the government, as no other nation before or since has ever done. All in all, moreover, America's period of global leadership was also both shorter and more insecure than was any previous leadership. How we will endure beyond this period is something we must now seriously ponder.

Recall that the United States was not a global power at all until a century ago. Only then did the United States take from the world as others, not long before, had taken from it. In part, America's delay in achieving world power was due to its youth, its immense geography, and its isolation from the rest of the world. Equally, however, it was due to America's pride in its isolation from global affairs. Although George Washington never actually used these words, Americans have followed what they took to be his admonition to beware of the perils of "foreign entanglements."

But if public foreign entanglements could not entice our involvement with the world, America's private interests, supported by a garrison here or a gunboat there, assumed it nonetheless. In some ways, this kind of entanglement was more amenable to the world than were those that came before it. This was because American colonialism was not prompted by the propagation of a faith or the demand for idle tribute. But in other ways, what America asked for—a place deep within the economy of other nations—was more intrusive than were incursions motivated by faith or the desire for tribute.

To be sure, America's private institutions never accounted for all that our country did in the world. At times, our worldly involvements were public, and some, including our contribution to the victories over authoritarian regimes in World War II, were both significant and laudable. What America has done to assist the victims of disasters or to provide food and medicine at times of famine and disease has been charitable and noteworthy. But just as an imbalance between our private and public interests has caused a reversal of our domestic fortunes, so too has the weakness of our public institutions for so long unbalanced our relations with the world in the private, economic direction.

Foreign governments, of course, traditionally have as much courted influence in the United States as our government has courted influence abroad. From the days of Benjamin Franklin's and Thomas Jefferson's ambassadorships to France and Citizen Genêt, international political influence has been reciprocally pursued by our government and others. But unlike other countries both today and in times past, the United States now is subject to an increased foreign influence not because of the smallness of our population or our people's poverty. We are subject to such influence because of the nature of our government and because of our recent history of permitting our own private interests to dominate it.

It was predictable that as our government has encouraged private interests to gather what they could from other nations, when America's fortunes turn downward, danger has come from other nation's private, as well as public, interests. The danger to America today stems not merely from the ability of the world's other governments to influence members of Congress, their staffs, the national bureaucracy, and other significant public institutions. The danger is as great as it is because of our government's vulnerability to *private* intrusions originating at home and abroad.

The New Form of Global Leadership

Apart from the increase of foreign private entanglements, another new form of influence has begun to affect America's international well-being. As the quality of global leadership changed when the United States assumed it, that quality is changing again as the next period of global stewardship begins. This new form of leadership, combining the private interests of many nations, has over recent years become more powerful than any single nation's overseas interest or any public or private interest combined in a single nation.

It is unfortunate that during its period of global leadership, the United States did not prepare for the next form. Enjoyment of our global dominance surely distracted us from consideration of what would have been both a more ennobling and a more secure global order once our period of ascendance was over. Curiously, the United States, in relation to the ever-growing global economy, finds itself in nearly the same circumstances as did America's individual states in their attempt to regulate the American economy 100 years ago. The difference, of course, is that the higher level involved today is not America's national government, but a still larger, but increasingly competitive, global economic structure.

What must America do to prepare itself better for the global age? Three areas of concern are relevant here. First, with regard to the citizens and nations of the Third World whom America dominated so readily in the past, the United States must insist upon a more equitable treatment of these peoples from those private interests that are potentially under American control. Such a commitment will require a public resolve to forestall the further enmity of those nations, who surely will turn against the United States when the issues of Third World debt, development, local wages and working conditions, and so on, become even more intensely debated than they currently are. It also requires that our government be able to enforce such a policy among our private interests. Can the government, for example, effectively restrain American tobacco interests from pushing their deadly products on the underdeveloped world? A commitment to this goal, although certainly moral, would be not solely a matter of charity toward the underdeveloped world. It would be a commitment, more importantly, to America's long-term global interest.

Second, as the course of the political world moves, happily, in the direction of democracy, it is imperative that the United States in particular encourage such movement even when it interferes with what America's private interests have found to be profitable in the undemocratic areas of the world. The type of democracy that we must promote in places such as Latin America, for example, must be founded on the same proper balance between private and public domains and between legal and political jurisdictions that we should promote in America. The mere existence of political candidacies and elections, of political parties of only narrow or no ideology, and of public institutions that though of apparent democratic form are easily manipulated by powerful private segments or the residue of recently authoritarian governments, does not represent true democracy. The forms of democracy in the rest of the world's nations are as meaningless without the balancing of preconstitutional considerations as they are here.

Third, with regard to the developed nations of the world and to those private interests that have combined in such a way as to attain truly international status, the position of the United States must be that access to its generous markets is contingent upon a global commitment to a balance of private-to-public influences. If one thing is clear today, it is that the unity of private interests throughout the world threatens more than the United States government and its people. As the world moves further into a stage wherein international private interests can and will dominate the global economy, the global political agenda, which is too seldom considered by national governments (and still not sufficiently represented by international institutions such as the United Nations), must now be addressed. The United States, before its international influence wanes still further, should take the lead in ensuring that global political concerns become enveloped in the kinds of global political institutions that will effectively and equitably deal with them.

In the final analysis, America's dealings with other nations must now encompass far more than the limited matter of how our private interests deal with the capital, the labor, and the raw materials of, say, the world's poorer regions. They must also transcend the question of how the technology, the management, and the human capital of other wealthy nations engage these resources. The coming together of the global economy necessitates nothing less than the coming together of the global political community. It also means that those who would retain their influence within the world and within the world's governments must offer and support a global standard of political equity.

It is a truism among those who study international relations that as the dominance, or hegemony, of a single international power declines, the need for international law—that is, the need for universally recognized standards of conduct—grows. International law soon will no longer be able to afford the luxury of the often arcane rulings that affect secondary international issues. A just world's requirement for the peaceful and self-determined survival of all nation-states and their peoples, whether they be powerful or not, requires a considerable growth of international law and a considerable strengthening of international organizations. In this regard, we must not forget that the improvement of what history will view as today's meager law of nations, along with the building of global institutions that refine and represent that law to the world, is in America's interest as much as it is in the interest of other nations.

Even within the context of a lawful and just world, during the new global period the ability of any nation to avoid economic and political vulnerability will be tested as never before. Ironically, the European nations, with governments that have proven capable of focusing their public policy so as to enhance their citizens' well-being, have chosen to protect their citizenry by participating more fully in the economies and the political decision making of other nations while at the same time surrendering a portion of their sovereignty to a regional political structure. In doing so, they have assured their future in the new global age far better than had they chosen to retain their outdated national sovereignties.

In contrast, the United States, which has guarded its national sovereignty more jealously than any other nation, has placed its citizenry at a greater risk of losing economic and even political sovereignty in the new global age by continuing to balkanize its political authority beyond what even the Framers intended. Whereas others have gathered their political structures in preparation for the new global age, the United States has accelerated the disassembling of its political structures into the tiny nationalities of congressional districts and senatorially represented states. In doing so, the United States has not only left itself more subject to private influence from abroad than other nations; it has also left our people less prepared than ever for the kinds of public decision making that will be required to forestall such intrusions.

During America's time of global leadership, the decentralized structure of its government may have fostered, or at least permitted, that kind of leadership to prosper and grow. Private national institutions, beyond the reach of our government in many instances, may have benefited the nation economically with what they were able to do abroad, unfettered by the government, even if their means of doing so were too often exploitative. But now, as the wheel of history turns, the disassembled government that so thoroughly invites access on behalf of domestic interests without challenge is now itself entangled by interests that come to it from outside America's borders. Those involuntary entanglements, expanding in the opposite direction from Washington's meanings and combined with the inability of our government to ensure the competitiveness of our nation's private domain, only hasten America's economic and political decline. They also hasten America's falling away from democracy. In doing so they deprive the world of the rightful contribution to democracy in an emerging global order that America can and should make.

11

The National Press

The Professional Ethic

No Washington institution is more purposefully divided in its role than is the national press. Walter Lippmann properly pointed out that the press was at one and the same time a part of and not a part of the government.[1] As the press should be an honest chronicler of the government's activities, Lippmann argued, it should also legitimately be an instrument through which the government informs its citizens of what it is that they should know.

Apart from deflecting government attempts either to prevent citizens from knowing what is true or to have them believe what is not true, the American press carries an additional burden in its governmental reporting. That burden begins with the nature of the American government itself, and particularly with the non-existence of a single entity that can properly be called the government. It extends into the field of journalistic ethics and how well journalists adhere to those ethics.

Each profession has its own set of ethical canons, but all professions adhere to a broad framework of universal ethical standards, the principal standard being that a professional's interests should never conflict with those of a client. Implicit in this standard is a deliberate separation of the served and the server, the agent and the principal. Proximity can undermine the service of any professional. The ethics of the national reporter require a distance from the government sufficient to ensure that the costs of covering the government do not fall on the public.

Of course, violations of professional standards of separation occur in all professions: doctors prescribe medicines to keep their patients well, but also to keep them as patients; lawyers sue when they should settle; and college professors, more than they admit, give agreeable grades to the students who fill their classes. Professionals have their own interests, and it is often tempting to conflate them with those of their clients. But the ambiguity of the national press's relationship to the national government confuses the professional standard in a unique way. The client is the reader—or the viewer or listener, in the case of the electronic media. But the press's relationship to its sources of information is so necessary to it that granting favorable coverage to that source is all too tempting.

What is it about the Framers' design of the American government that makes the prostitution of its press coverage more likely than it is anywhere else? For one thing, the dispersion of the American government means that some portion of that government is nearly always in conflict with another portion. The division between the executive and the legislative branches, particularly when Republicans and Democrats have held those branches separately for so long, is only the most obvious of these divisions.

The divisions that exist throughout the government mean that governmental actors at all levels will advocate the positions of their jurisdictions in the hope of maintaining their segmented prerogatives more vigorously than they would in an integral government. Endemic in the American arrangement is a willingness on the part of each component to "leak" information to the press in order to provide confidential information as to what will happen in the government. There is also a particular eagerness to provide unfriendly information about jurisdictional rivals. The national press, unfortunately, is rarely reluctant to use such information, regardless of its source or motivation, particularly if such usage helps maintain access to a source. The national reporter's information about the government subtly becomes information that distends the government—this occurring, incidentally, without the client's— the reader's, the viewer's, or the listener's—understanding. As the press grows closer to the parts of the government, the relationship of the press with the client is estranged. Lippmann's balances are thus clearly betrayed in favor of the government.

Beyond the estrangement of the citizenry from its right to information, a further cost accrues from the press's failure to maintain a professional balance. Curiously, in its attempt to obtain governmental information, the press has developed a manner of relating to its sources of information that reinforces the principal interactions of the government. In a government as dispersed as America's, the dominance of contract-like decision structures such as those connecting interests and contributors with compliant legislators has meant that the supplier of information to the press—the source—imposes the government's contractual form on the press. And the press, by accepting information in that form, becomes little more than a link in what Washington calls its "networks." Over time, as governmental sources expect to come and too often do come to "understandings" with the press, compliance by the press with the contractual form of receiving its information reinforces the contractual manner of governmental interaction. Put another way, as the press accepts that part of its role that makes it so much a part of government through its own contracting, it not incidentally ratifies the very governmental dispersion that made it easier for the press to be compromised in the beginning. The truth is that the forms of doing business that now pervade the American government have received their greatest rein-forcement from the national press—even, at times, from those who honestly attempt to report on the government objectively.

Inevitably, as reinforcement of governmental dispersion marks the press's reporting on the government, it also marks how the press reports on the entire government's performance. Too much of what the press reports in its descriptions of how the govern-ment works in fact describes how the government does *not* work. The excessive patterning of centrifugal over centripetal decision structures and the dominance of the contractual "networking" governmental form over the processes of aggregation that have been increasingly winnowed from the American government are the kinds of developments that the public should most know about. Predictably, they hear very little about it.

A Washington Standard

What, then, should the standard of ethical obligation for the na-tional press be now that the government has undergone such substantial structural change? And how should the national press report on the new preconstitutional arrangements of the national government in keeping with that professional standard? Here Lippmann is relevant again, for as the Washington press is both a part of and not a part of the government, the definition of a professional standard for it is more imperative than ever. Both the ancient Biblical standard and the standard of the law of agency in the British common law command that no one can serve two masters.

If the press is to be the handmaiden of government in telling a citizenry what the government is doing, and if the press is also to be the servant of the citizenry in its defense against the govern-ment, which loyalty comes first? The answer is not difficult, for the very reason that the proper relationship of any democratic government to its citizens is itself not difficult. The press's first loyalty is to the citizenry, not because of any necessary preference among the press for the citizenry, but, again, because the *government's* first loyalty is to the citizenry. The press's loyalty only naturally follows the proper political order.

Overall, therefore, the press serves its clients best by being as detached from the parts of its government as it can be. Admittedly, that detachment is far more easily proposed than achieved. The incentive is always there, even in a degree among the most integrated of governments, to obtain information by proximity to some part of that government. But is it not reasonable to expect that in interchanges with any part of the government, a reporter should ask how that singular, often self-seeking perspective fits or does not fit into the entire government? This is how the press might best represent the government and uphold the first half of Lippmann's obligation without disturbing its principal obligation to the citizenry.

In speaking in this manner for the entire American government, the press's inquiries into any portion of it could also contribute to a sense of urgency concerning the government's recent failures. Any source with which the reporter interacts should be reminded not only that the recent record of American governmental performance has been unacceptable but also that the public, as a part of the reporter's charge, must now be made aware of the government's failures.

In sum, the obligation of the American press to report on the government's recent failures is both more imperative and more obvious now than ever. In communicating with the reader, viewer, or listener, reporters covering the United States government must now do far more than relate the status of contemporary, substantive issues that stand before the government, even such important issues as those concerning the budget deficit, the trade imbalance, and so forth. Washington reporting must now include a conscious discussion of the ways in which such crucial public issues have recently been avoided by the government. Even though the substantive information that a Washington reporter receives is frequently relayed in the context of the source's political advancement, conveying an understanding of how the sources of government in Washington have estranged the government from its principal obligation must now be a part of any Washington political reporting.

In reporting on news within the framework of a government that has grown more dispersed than it was ever planned to be and in candidly reporting on the government's recent failures, the Washington reporter is in a position to accomplish something of considerable significance for the American people. The national press must now act as an active counterbalance to the structural dispersion and the all-too-convenient political finger-pointing of the national government that has allowed Washington's officeholders to escape responsibility for their actions and inactions. Put another way, the Washington reporter, rather than ratify how the government works or does not work, must begin to question the unstated and now inaccurate assumptions of successful government that Washington officeholders and staff members, for obvious reasons, wish to have the press advance.

As argued earlier, although the Washington press is both of the government and not of the government, the press's relationship with the reader is infinitely more important than the press's relationship with the government. The recent distortions of the structure of the American national government and the pulling of all too many of Washington's reporters into the orbit of the government's dispersions have led to an inability, and on the part of many an unwillingness, to expose, much less protest against, the structural changes that have distorted the government's pre-constitutional balances. As a result, the American public has not only suffered the consequences of the recent changes in the unwritten constitution, but it has also suffered the obscuring of these changes by one of the two institutions (the other being the academy) that should be addressing them most forthrightly.

Let us not forget, either, that the most important impact of the recent changes in the American government has not been that on the public official, as some have suggested. The most significant effect of these changes has been that on the relationship between the American people and their government. As that relationship has been distorted in recent years, American democracy has suffered accordingly.

Thus, as a doctor should prescribe honestly for a patient and as a lawyer should give unselfish advice to a client, the national press now more than ever should uphold the independent standards of its profession rather than yield to those upon whom it relies for immediate professional sustenance. Any reporter covering the national government must now report on both the reality and the meaning of what has recently happened to the American government. To be sure, this will not always make for easy work, for it certainly will not gratify those who have become familiar sources within the government. Neither will it gratify those in the press who have found it convenient for so long not to go beyond such sources. Nonetheless, as the American government has altered itself so dramatically in the last years, and as it has altered itself largely to accommodate those who hold office within it and those private interests who have won public favor through it, the Washington reporter who adheres most honestly to journalism's ethical standard is the reporter who will report on exactly what has happened. This is what democracy has always required of its press and what it requires now more than ever.

Note

1. Richard Steele, *Propaganda in an Open Society, The Roosevelt Administration and the Media, 1933–1941.* New York: Greenwood Press, 1985.

12

The Academy

Structure and Role

No nongovernmental institutions are more important to the long-term well-being of this country than are America's institutions of higher learning. For all of their importance, however, our universities and colleges are highly vulnerable institutions. Their roles and indeed their very structures are subject, as a result, to a more considerable degree of prostitution than is any nongovernmental, or perhaps even governmental, entity.

The long-term significance of the modern American university transcends the traditional university role of educating the next generation. It even goes beyond the Platonic notion of the socialization of each generation into the ratification of the culture and the norms of the political society. Nothing less than the way in which the next generation understands the dilemmas of the future, nothing less than a disciplined teaching of that set of mental and spiritual tools that gives the next generation a fair opportunity to resolve those dilemmas, is at stake in the modern American university.

When it functions properly, a university is far more than a contributor to the accumulation of knowledge. What a properly functioning university does, quietly but unmistakably, is to contribute to the building of those original intellectual frameworks in which each generation's novel problems are first understood and subsequently dealt with. The university's role in a democratic society, therefore, is more than that of a repository of substantive knowledge. Its training of America's next generation either assures or vitiates the university's ability to define our society's most difficult political choices.

There are, of course, two kinds of universities, private and public. By and large, private universities, although historically charged with considerable responsibility for furthering the public well-being, have been allowed to place themselves, if they wished, farther from the public charge than the public university. The private university, in a sense, is already owned. It is already committed, financially and otherwise, to a selection of intellectual interests. It may even be committed, if it wishes, to a perspective on those interests that is akin to what the private economic forces that have supported its agenda—and have properly expected to receive some benefit from that agenda—have long encouraged.

The public university, in contrast, can and must be a different entity. The most considerable public concerns of the nation must be discussed there even if they are not discussed in any other institution. Yet as universities both private and public are little more than a loose collection of necessarily semiautonomous colleges, departments, and even individual faculty members, the threat to the public charge of the public university has grown to the point where it frequently is no more public-spirited than are the interest-dominated private universities.

The major issue faced by the public university today, in terms of its structure and role, is that its quiet wholeness, that aggregat-

ing of its disparate parts, must more than ever contend with its
vocal and self-interested parts. Those parts, which reflect the
interests that have responded to forces coming from outside the
university, are fully contented with the university's gangliness.
Indeed, some of the university's internal actors, though they
would never admit it, find themselves more comfortable with
what would influence the university from the outside than with
assuming their agenda-setting and citizenship-preparing role for
the next generation.

The University's Charge

In modern public universities, sadly, something has recently happened concerning the struggle between the university's whole
and its parts that is more threatening to it, and to the country,
than anything that has happened before. What has happened is
that the very offices within the public university that are in the
best position to maintain its public structure and role have become more vulnerable to outside, interest-related pressures than
have any other corners of those universities. It is the administration of the university, not the faculty, that must constitute the
institution's wholeness. Yet it is the administration, in its onerous
bearing of the burden of competing with both private and other
public universities in what is surely a marketplace for faculty,
students, research support, public acceptance and the like, that
has become less protective of the wholeness of the university
than at any time in the history of the public school. The administrators of a public university, unlike the faculty, must compete
for funding that is never wholly adequate for the school because
of the school's competition with the entire panoply of public
agencies and institutions that come before state legislatures.

As a result, what should be the most integral segment of a
university, its administrative leadership, is now often the most

likely to divert the university from its most sacred public charge. Sadly, the public university has become increasingly prone to offer itself in recent years to those private interests in its community, such as the defense industry, who are most desirous and most capable of purchasing the services that in many cases only public universities provide.

What should a public university and particularly its administrators do to forestall this current momentum toward the devolution of public universities into discrete, marketable divisions? What makes a public university more than an institution that is merely responsive to those outside, private interests that would prostitute its public role? Three postures suggest themselves for the public university, each designed for the maintenance of its larger historical mission in a way that should never be negotiable.

First, the modern public university must maintain the broadest possible sense of the common good. The public university's unique educational contribution to the citizenry's well-being must define a broader scope of potential considerations of public concern than that offered by any other private or public institution in America. Private educational institutions, by virtue of their more immediate concern with pursuits that contribute directly to their own existence, will delimit the scope of their concern to such pursuits. The public university, in a consciously complementary fashion if necessary, must concern itself with what is, and even with what only might be, in the nation's broadest *future* public interest without undue consideration of immediate claims upon it.

Second, the public university, and particularly its administrators, must be mindful of the natural bias that comes with the courting of private and even certain public monies. It is no easy feat, to be sure, to encourage support for a university among those who surely wish something from it and then treat those interests without favor in the grander allocations of the university. But if it cannot be ended, intellectual and departmental bias within the public university must be at least minimized, if for no other reason than the fact that such bias will almost invariably penalize those intellectual areas that are the least able to provide the most immediate return to society.

Principally affected, of course, are the liberal arts, where the core of each generation finds its most innovative leadership and where any society's most important public values are engendered, defined, and made available for public consideration. The compensatory nature of any university administration's leadership in upholding this less immediately rewarding university interest is clear. But the determination of the level of support for various programs within the university must reflect both the integrity of the university as a whole and its respect for the long-term and broad-gauge benefits of the liberal disciplines.

Third, the public university, more so perhaps than any other public institution, must maintain an openness about its dealings with the public and the private institutions with which it interacts. The costs of secrecy in a public educational institution are enormous. The university's funding and attention are more readily diverted to nonpublic and short-term pursuits when that diversion is hidden from the faculty, the student population, and, most importantly, the citizenry. The commitments of a public university must never be hidden from the public, for it is the public that should have the final, democratically guaranteed prerogative over the direction of its educational institutions.

It should be no surprise that the hiding of the decision making of a public university's priorities often goes hand-in-hand with subtle discriminations among the faculty over who is willing and who is not willing to participate in the task of responding to external interests. It is no secret either that knowledge of the secretiveness of future decision-making processes concerning such allocations encourages silence among the faculty in the necessary debate over university goals.

Secrecy in a public university thus not only diverts the attention of the university's administration from maintaining the proper balance of concerns. Secrecy presents an even more serious and direct threat to the university's public character itself. If private, external interests wish to engage segments of the public university for their immediate and often profitable use, the secrecy of that purchase facilitates, more than anything else, the loss of that methodology which may account for a balance among the university's missions. When the contractual arrangements that private interests push on a willing public university are kept secret, in other words, the university and the general public both lose their means of accounting for the university's public mission. The secreting of a public university's decision processes is as undemocratic as is the secreting of any public institution's decision processes. It should never be allowed.

The Problem of the Foundation

Virtually all universities today, both private and public, support and in turn are supported by, extra-institutional foundations or institutes. These foundations or institutes can be and certainly have been helpful to America's universities serving as conduits through which important contributions have been made to the larger educational mission of their schools. But as these ancillary foundations or institutes have settled in beside the nation's major public universities, while usually operating under the legal protection granted to other private, nonprofit corporations, they have intruded upon as well as assisted in the funding of faculty and research assistant salaries, laboratory equipment, and the like.

Though advertised as being designed for the general good of the university, the fact is that too often these foundations have fallen under the influence of a small number of anonymous, private contributors who, were they to contribute directly to the university's general fund, would not be permitted to purchase what they are able to purchase secretly. This secret prostitution of the university's general public mission ultimately leads to a kind of a prostitution of the public nature of the university. The citizenry, in a sense, is outbid for control of its own institution and the very bidding for the institution itself is done secretly, without public knowledge or acceptance.

As a result, the public loses twice when the ancillary foundation secrets private monies and furthers private interests through the public university. It loses the judgment and services of those administrators who should work for the public exclusively but who no longer do so because their services have been purchased by the foundation's contributors. It loses again as the very public nature of the institution that it supports in the good faith understanding that university administrators are working for the public good and not for those who have secretly bought into the enterprise is corrupted by those who have been hired in a fiduciary capacity vis-à-vis the institution. The public depends upon its public universities as its most effective safeguard of the future well-being of the nation. The subtle, piecemeal transition of public universities into what promises to become increasingly private educational institutions is a dangerous and a foreboding reality. It is the ancillary university foundation that has been the nose under the tent with regard to this subtle transition.

In the final analysis, among all of the significant institutions of a democracy, the public university is the last and in many ways the best bulwark of the public interest. Ironically, although it must be largely apolitical in its public posture, it must courageously uphold the public interest in what is, in one sense at least, an openly political way. The final products of democracy— its elections, its political parties, its political discourse, and even its patently political institutions—such as Congress and the presidency in the United States—trace their democratic nature to that saltmarsh of democratic ideals that must be regenerated, more than anywhere else, in the nation's public universities.

The sale of that portion of the saltmarsh that belongs in the public universities to developers of immediate and individual gain—with private universities already under unabashed influence—imperils the ability of these universities to prepare the nation's next generation for democratic solutions to the public dilemmas it will face. The struggle for a proper balance of private and public interest in a free society neither begins nor ends with the government. It begins, and ends, within what must be the most regenerative institution of any free society—its universities. Thomas Jefferson's admonitions concerning the linkage between public education and the future of American democracy are as relevant today as when he spoke them.

Clearly, then, the people who are trustees for the public universities of the United States, those who have in their care the embryonic frameworks of solutions for problems not yet understood and not yet even a part of the American democracy's political dialogue, must withstand the seductive influence of interests who would divert the university away from those considerations to what is more immediate, more visible, and often far more rewarding. No institution in America presents a greater disparity between its true interest and the pressures it sustains from those with whom it interacts than does the public university. Management of that disparity, however, is absolutely indispensable to the maintenance of the public university's most valuable contribution to our country.

13

Remedies

The Citizen and Public Imbalance

If the United States is to recover its political respect among the democratic nations of the world, it must first remedy those things within its government that have made this country less democratic than it once was. To initiate such remedies, it is not sufficient merely to consider a variety of constitutional and preconstitutional alterations of the government's recent restructuring. There is a sequence to reform, and, short of a dramatic and more than likely uncontrollable series of ill-considered changes in the government that would be anything but desirable, the strategy for structural reform must be as well-considered as the substance of reform. Within the outline of America's present constitutional order, and within the outline of democracy that all enlightened nations properly acknowledge today, the American people can and must engender change in their government through a moderate, evolutionary process.

As with all matters of undoing what has been done over a considerable period, no single order of change is likely to be agreed upon by all. Public consideration should therefore be given to which among a variety of potential strategies best accomplishes the reversal of America's democratic decline. It may seem advisable to some, for example, to retrace the evolution of the preconstitutional imbalances that led to the American decline in what they perceive to be the reverse order of the decline. It is not at all clear, however, which institutions and practices began America's governmental imbalances; indeed, it is altogether likely that all of the government's principal institutions were afflicted more or less simultaneously. Retracing the steps of the imbalance, therefore, is not a plausible remedial strategy.

From another perspective, it may seem advisable to examine first those institutions that are deemed most central to the American government. But there is no agreement over which institutions are most central, and the squabbles among our institutions over their relative centrality have, in fact, been a principal factor in the decline. Also, it seems clear that each of America's principal political institutions has been a part of the governmental decline. The cure of one segment alone would not forestall reinfection from the uncured segments.

The best strategy for the reform of the American government, therefore, may be to follow the sequence in which democratic principles and the political enterprises of a democratic government normally function. The flow of democracy, in other words, should serve as the flow of democracy's reform. Accordingly, it is the people who should first address the issue of their government's de-democratization. It is the people, with the assistance of those in the academy, those who seek public office who are truly disposed to help the people, those in the press and those from other sectors of the American society that are so inclined, who must initiate America's structural reform.

Structural reform will not be an easy task. Indeed, the task is even more difficult today than it would have been only a short time ago because the disparity between what is ideal and what is real in the American political process has grown a good deal recently. Another complicating factor is that a considerable quantity of misinformation about the government, proffered largely by national officeholders and by the ancillary Washington institutions that cater to them, has lately confused the public with regard to the processes under which the government operates. As a result, the American citizenry is less certain of how its government works and less resolved upon the ideal of how it should work in the context of the current state of the nation than it has ever been before. For all that, however, the American citizenry is generally, if imprecisely, aware that its government has not acted as it should in recent years. From that awareness, the citizenry may be able to begin work toward meaningful reform.

Inevitably, although the entire public must be given an opportunity to inform itself of the government's difficulties, some Americans will be more willing than others to consider evidence of the recent decline and thus work for reform. But whatever portion of our citizenry has such an understanding and such a willingness to work must not be deterred from initiating remedial action merely because the entire polity is not so disposed. Further, no citizen should be deterred from initiating remedial action because there is no immediate consensus on the avenue of reform. The early stages of political reform throughout history have necessarily been irregular and spontaneous. But irregularity and spontaneity have always been the catalysts of the most creative solutions to problems, not distractions from them.

The Political Party

Apart from the public's individual efforts and the assistance that the public should receive from the academy, the media, and the willing office seeker, the first public institution that should assist in the quest for structural reform is the American political party. The political party, particularly the Democratic Party, has an opportunity with this issue to reclaim its standing as the regenerative conduit between the public and the government. The interest group, along with the ancillary governmental institutions of the Beltway, the elections industry, and the Washington lawyer-lobbyist that have recently altered the government, must now be balanced by the one potentially aggregative institution that has most clearly been circumvented in recent years by these disaggregating institutions.

If the American people are reasonably to expect the level of governmental integrity that comes with those who govern maintaining a Burkean distance from those who are governed, America's parties must first achieve that degree of internal integrity that will permit them to counter the individuated demands that have recently kept them from channeling public policies to the government. A program for structural reform can come only from those who are in a position to consider the varied requirements of the American citizenry without the frequent and immediate insistence of each interest that its individual political demands be met. The parties are the first institution that should do this.

In the context of what is still an embryonic discussion of constitutional reform around the country, the convening of a national constitutional convention has been suggested by some. For a variety of reasons, including but not limited to those considerations of politics and party mentioned above, a general constitutional convention is not in the best interest of the country or of America's political parties. In the spirit of what our political parties should be, however, an avenue is open for a *party* convention role in governmental reform. That avenue should be taken, at least by the Democratic Party.

The convening of true party policy conventions should have taken place in the United States a long time ago. These conventions should have included the legislative and, if applicable, executive leadership among each party's national officeholders. They should also have included fair representation for a variety of citizen's groupings as well as for those individuals who seek a purpose and direction for our parties rather than the furtherance of a particular interest. Ideally, in the near future, conventions of each party will meet and address themselves solely to the issue of constitutional reform.

Whatever constitutional remedies are proposed by the party conventions, it is clear that statutorally generated electoral reform is also essential for the re-democratization of our government. Both of America's parties, in the context of their sequential role in governmental reform, must assist the American people in accomplishing the dual tasks of (a) increasing the public share of funding for America's congressional campaigns and (b) funneling such financing through the national political parties. Mere disclosure of funding sources will never ensure electoral, much less governmental, reform. The mere closure of loopholes in funding laws that now permit "soft" money to be funneled from individuals and interests to candidates through quasi-political organizations and other front institutions will not ensure electoral reform, either.

True reform will come to the American political system only when successful candidates are required to adhere reasonably well to the platform of the party from which they have received funding. The disparate interests that have so weakened America's parties, in league with the officeholders who currently benefit from their alliances with those interests, will almost certainly oppose a reform of this nature. Only the full participation of the parties themselves, implemented through such devices as the party convention, will assure that that kind of reform takes place.

One more consideration bears mention with regard to America's political parties and their role in the rebalancing of America's political institutions. Although local circumstances should and always will play a significant role in the selection of candidates who run for high office, the leadership of each of America's major parties must play a more active role in the recruitment throughout the country of congressional candidates who will speak to the issue of structural reform. If America's political parties are to be effective aggregators of public policy, it is no longer desirable for national parties to play as small a part as they have recently in the selection of those candidates for public office who are properly expected to further the party's national position. This is true particularly in Congress. And, with regard to structural reform, the parties' active support for candidates who will courageously speak to this vital issue is more important still.

The Congressional Member

In the proper sequence of what an effective and democratic political system should provide for its citizenry, the institution that most directly responds to the aggregated preferences that political parties present to it is the legislature. The legislature that takes *party* positions, not merely the position that results from some random aggregation of the positions of individual legislators, and molds those positions into public law is an effective and democratic legislature. With regard to the internal changes that Congress needs to make, as well as with regard to other structural changes in the government, the membership of Congress, and particularly the congressional leadership, should welcome the opportunity to participate in the party conventions we have discussed.

The leadership position that members of the legislature would be assured of in the policy-oriented conventions that America's parties should hold in future years and that both members and leaders must assume in the early, structurally directed conventions of the immediate future should be attractive to the legislative leadership for a variety of reasons. Freed from the procedural constraints of the House and Senate, freed from the opposition of congressional members of the other party, and, freed from the attention that is given to the presidential nominating process in the current quadrennial conventions, legislative members should feel comfortable in a convention that is focused on strategies for structural reform. They should also feel a sense of obligation with regard to their participation in such a party conference, much as the legislative members of parties throughout Europe willingly view such participation as properly attendant to their public responsibility.

As mentioned before, legislators of both parties have repeatedly decried the excessive costs of recent campaigns. The almost perpetual need for fund-raising that besets these campaigns and the deleterious effect that the necessary investment of time for such fund-raising has had on their ability to focus on the public agenda have cost Congress and the country dearly. Some legislators have publicly acknowledged that the pattern of their fund-raising has limited the scope of their legislative considerations. In view of the need to please so many interests within the venue of the legislative session who are, invariably, also contributors, a party convention may be the only venue within which the congressional member can refute those who have suggested that their recent protestations over money and influence are insincere. A convention can give each member an opportunity to devise protections from those interests that now so easily have access to the congressional member.

Beyond constitutional reforms and statutorily generated electoral reform, a party convention could also provide members of Congress with an opportunity to confer about a number of reforms of the internal arrangements of Congress. For example, members could consider a review of current allocations of staffing responsibility, specifically whether additions to leadership ranks and party staff can be made at the expense of the overblown personal staffs that members of Congress have recently made available to themselves. They could also consider an increase in the authority of party leadership within the legislative houses at the expense of committee jurisdictions as well as an increase in the role that the party caucuses play in ensuring the development of policy positions within Congress.

As argued earlier, the legislature is the lifeblood of any democracy. It was the power of legislature—the popular legislature—that constitutional-era democrats such as the antifederalists sought to protect from dilution in the constitutional arrangement. Along with internal reform, therefore, a restoration of the balance between America's legislative and executive jurisdictions is one of the primary reforms that current congressional members, and particularly the current congressional leadership, should address in a party convention.

Sadly, the recently disassembled Congress has demonstrated that its members cannot labor within the Burkean tradition of the trusted repositor of the public good. A convening of a party convention made up of each party's legislative members along with other interested party members may offer the only way to encourage consideration of reform of the internal disassemblings of Congress, the difficulties of electoral financing, and the constitutional imbalance between the legislative and the executive branches. America's legislators should take the opportunity of a party convention to remedy all of these imbalances and thus resume the role of the trusted protector of democracy that the antifederalists wanted the American legislature to fulfill.

One final point with regard to Congress and its members. In the recent past, a clamor for a restriction of legislative terms has gone up among a public justifiably outraged with the performance of its government. Initiatives of this nature have actually succeeded at the state level. Though the logic of the proponents' argument bears relevance to the difficulties of the federal legislature, the suggested cure is, unfortunately, worse than the disease. What is wrong with Congress is not the longevity of the members who serve within it. It is the lack of electoral vulnerability of those who serve, whether for a short or a long time. Rather than place an arbitrary limit upon the service of members of Congress, it may well be time for Congress, instead of the state governments, to draw lines of congressional representation that are truly competitive and that will more truly reflect the political wishes of the American people as a whole rather than the most provincial wishes of each of the country's electoral segments.

The Local Contribution

Traditional understandings of America's complex government, with their obligatory distinctions among the levels of government, detract from a more precise understanding of the nation's political condition. That understanding must take into account the increasing inability of the government to reconcile its local, county, state, and federal jurisdictions. First, with regard to the role of subnational governments, more than a modern-day extension of a contractual understanding or a "marble cake" understanding or even a partnership understanding among America's vertical jurisdictions is now needed. Nothing less than a thorough redefinition of the levels of the various American governments must be undertaken. Traditional definitions of the levels of government in America are far less important today, and, surely, far less representative of the way that America's publics actually constitute themselves than they have ever been before.

Thorough reform of the American government, therefore, can occur only after the people of this country inform themselves of the need for reform both at the federal level and at the level of government closest to them. If governmental reform is to be meaningful in this country, local reforms, similar in spirit to those that must be initiated at the national level, must redefine the local governmental order.

The current plethora of local governments—school boards, special service districts, suburban corporations, counties, etc.— unmercifully confuses both local government generally and the people's preferences for local government policy specifically. At the local level, much as at the national level, this confusion is first manifested by a diminishing of the public's sense of what should rightfully be expected from government. Only the high visibility of the national government has made its recent confusion of authority more obvious to the citizen than that of the local governments. But the local confusion is every bit as serious. Further, the high visibility of the national government has at least begun to reveal to the citizenry the cost of national-level fragmentation, while it has thus far masked the damage caused by local-government fragmentation. The metropolitan coordination of police and fire protection, the guarantee of a sound public education, and the provision of water, sewer, health, and other necessary services suffer as never before from the dreadful inefficiencies caused by the fragmentation of local government. Even more ominously, they suffer from the increasing lack of equity that is evident across major metropolitan areas in the delivery of such services.

The Local Strategy

As a result, the best strategy for the remedying of local government fragmentation would mirror that for the remedying of the federal government. Rather than a national party convention, however, the cities of America should hold a national urban convention, attended by selected citizens of large urban areas

throughout the United States, these cities' mayors, their representatives in Congress, and those who are genuinely concerned with
these cities' welfare. This convention should make the case that
the calculus of discriminatory political activity that was imposed
on municipal jurisdictions by their states at the beginning of this
century has reached full fruition and that a redefinition of the
urban area itself is therefore needed. The state governments'
ready incorporation of suburbs, their intentional failure to reapportion legislative districts so as to represent fairly the central
cities, and their restriction of what would have been natural an-
nexations to the central cities have, over the century, placed
America's urban areas in what is now a clearly untenable political position. How that position can be reversed must be the topic
of a national urban convention.

It is important to remember that previous attempts to assist the
central cities, even when honestly ventured, have never addressed the relationship of urban areas to America's other governments. Attempts to help the cities have hinged on initiatives
such as revenue sharing, apportioned expenditure, and block
grants that, even though often instigated at the local level, were
only ratified and funded at the federal level. Under such programs, unfortunately, the structural inequities that have been vis-
ited on America's cities throughout this century were only
ratified. But if traditional understandings of the levels of
America's governments are as arbitrary and as debilitating as this
century's discriminations have proven them to be, a solution to
the universal problems of our central cities must be initiated by
local governments that are prepared to make a general constitutional argument as part of their specific requests for federally
generated program funding.

In November 1990, the mayors of America's thirty-five largest
cities held an unprecedented meeting in New York. That meeting
should be repeated annually until such time as the routinized and

institutionalized business of those cities is developed to the degree that a call for a national urban convention will be credible and have a real chance of placing the cities' constitutional argument before the American people.

The constitutional argument the cities must bring before the American people and the national government should be supported by both a legal and a political strategy. The legal strategy should build upon existing federal law that mandates comparable funding for a variety of public services. The Supreme Court has already held that states are in violation of the Fourteenth Amendment's guarantee of the equal protection of the laws when they permit discriminatory funding of entities like the public schools. It is time now for the cities of America to engage in a broad range of legal challenges to the funding maldistributions that afflict virtually every public service that local governments provide throughout America's metropolitan areas. Again, the seedbed of early-twentieth-century state government discrimination against the cities has borne its bitter fruit to the degree that an equal protection argument is now both plausible and just as a means of redress.

In the legal arena as well, the cities should remember that in one of the cases that former Chief Justice Earl Warren considered to be the most important of his tenure, *Brown* v. *Board of Education*, the Court held that separation of the races in America's public schools was inherently unequal. Today, America's courts should be presented with cases that speak to the separations—racial, economic, and otherwise—that have surely increased throughout this century between America's cities and their suburbs. More than at any other time in the past twenty-five years, the isolated citizenry that lives within the arbitrary central-city jurisdiction is deprived by their states of its natural relationship with those around them. Though the Warren-era Supreme Court spoke boldly in the 1960s to the unfairness of urban political representation in cases like *Baker* v. *Carr* and *Reynolds* v. *Sims*, the impact of these cases was considerably less significant than was the impact of *Brown*. They came, unfortunately, only after large populations had already moved out of the cities. As it was the suburbs and not the cities that gained from *Baker* and its progeny, the cities and their friends are entitled now to correct that deprivation through further legal action.

As for the political portion of the cities' strategy, it is of more than passing interest to note that the antifederalist position during the constitutional period was better represented in Virginia than in any other state. Today, Virginia, alone among the states, has a system of local government in which cities are not only not politically subordinate to counties but, as cities' natural expansion occurs, the state permits the cities to extend their boundaries into the necessarily eroded county jurisdictions.

To be sure, a sprinkling of other states have permitted their cities to expand in somewhat more facilitative ways than some years ago. But all too few states have encouraged such innovations as the use of the original county boundary for the new home of the entire metropolitan jurisdiction. More importantly, the national government has never been involved in the expansion of the cities because the national government still declines to extend its authority to the matter of the internal corporate jurisdictions of the states. Therefore, as a complement to the legal strategy outlined above, America's city governments should demand that the national government now address itself to the legal separation of the central city from its state-protected suburbs. As argued earlier, America's cities must no longer be the exclusive province of the states. The injustices that they have suffered at the hands of their states, and the misfortunes that their citizens have suffered as a result of those injustices, require federal action and, perhaps, federal jurisdictional sovereignty, particularly in the matter of defining today's appropriate metropolitan boundaries.

In sum, because 80 percent of Americans now live in this

country's metropolitan regions and because the central cities are now lapsing into ever greater economic difficulty and political impotence, one of the goals of the urban convention proposed earlier should be the drafting of a constitutional amendment that pointedly overturns the state discriminations of the early part of the century and remedies the results of those discriminations. The entire set of issues dealing with the allocation of public funding resources along with the even more important set of issues concerning metropolitan boundaries and the jurisdictional prerogatives of those who make those boundaries must be on the agenda of such a convention. Appropriate federal legislation in the area of municipal boundaries is long overdue, and such legislation must be generated by those who have suffered legal and political discrimination throughout the twentieth century.

In the broad view, the fragmentations that afflict America's municipal governments and those that afflict national government are nowhere near so different, or so disconnected, as they may at first appear. Further, the imbalances of centrifugal and centripetal forces of artificially differentiated levels of government have also impacted dangerously on the other preconstitutional balances of private-to-public, legal-to-political, and majoritarian-to-antimajoritarian influences at each level of America's governments.

To remedy one level of governmental ills without remedying the others, or to prescribe remedies to one without consideration of those remedies' impact on the others will not reverse America's recent governmental fragmentation and its attendant de-democratization. Any understanding of America's current governmental difficulties must include a sure sense of the governmental imbalances that exist at all of America's increasingly deeply intertwined levels of public authority. It must also include a remedy for each of these level's imbalances.

14

Jefferson's and Lincoln's Lessons

The Democratic Standard

The injustices that George III imposed on his American colonists, by any historical standard of colonial suppression, were almost benign. It would have been simple—as, indeed, many colonists preferred—to have paid the petty tribute of a tea tax and continue living under what was far less than onerous rule. Those who rebelled against the British king did so only because their standard of democracy was so high.

Although they preferred to speak of it in practical as well as in philosophical terms, what the rebellious American colonists claimed for themselves was nothing less than a new standard of democracy. That standard, which is now part of what liberal democracy, as a political philosophy, offers to the world, centered on guarantees of the individual rights of a citizen and the right of the citizenry as a whole to a democratic government. Those guarantees must not only be reemphasized but improved upon in America's third century.

As the colonists' case against the king was not exceptional, it needed all the more to be rooted in a deep sense of justice. Equally, those who feel that the American political system today falls short of democracy must root their case deeply in what democracy itself both is and must become in the immediate future. We renew democracy best by understanding the too often unstated balances that are its preconditions. We develop new standards for democracy by looking both behind and beyond the old.

What has happened to the American government in recent years has been discussed in the preceding pages. The preconstitutional balances that exist between our private and public domains, and between our legal and political jurisdictions, as well as our other preconstitutional balances, have been markedly disturbed. The public's growing inability to bring majoritarian proposals before Congress has weakened the legislature, and the government as a whole, immeasurably. The growing dominance of legal over political representation has done nothing less than change the informal, if not the formal, character of the American government.

Within America's tradition of limited government, restrictions on political activity have traditionally been complemented by First Amendment protections of public, majoritarian access to the government. The antifederalist tradition and its central contribution of the Bill of Rights lie at the core of the democratic guarantee of public debate and decision making.

What has happened to both the private-to-public balance and the legal-to-political balance is that, as mentioned throughout, the structure of the government has been extended to institutions that operate outside the Constitution's design. The Beltway consultant, the lawyer-lobbyist, and the elections industry consultant have pushed our government's institutions beyond where they were intended to be. The intersection of our government with those institutions that now possess at least a quasi-public character has not had the effect of extending the public sphere, however. To the contrary, that intersection has allowed an extension of the private domain into the government. The resultant inability of the government to tend to the public's business in any aggregative way has permitted the further growth of these influential institutions. Moreover, it has carried private decision making back through the overextended channels of government to the public core. As a result, the United States government has become little more than a collection of nonaggregated, essentially contractual, relationships. These relationships add up to something far less than a democratic government.

The Tensions of History

Recall Jefferson's admonition that each generation must revitalize the nation's Constitution. It is as powerful an admonition today as it was then. Only one American public figure has had a greater impact upon America's politics than Thomas Jefferson. That figure is Abraham Lincoln. Though it was Jefferson who more than any president built the institutions of American democracy by usage, it was Lincoln who saw our nation through its greatest crisis, the deepest separation among its peoples. That separation, of course, resulted in the American Civil War.

The division that led to the Civil War was regionally based. The two grand geographical sections of our nation had divided themselves with their warring words in Congress and elsewhere long before Lincoln's presidency. Eventually, the nation was held together by Lincoln's words and deeds—and not just those words and deeds that led to the successful prosecution of the war. In promising "malice towards none and charity for all" in his second inaugural address at the same time that he promised a vigorous prosecution of the war, Lincoln stood for a generous coming together of the nation after the conflict. He purposefully chose words of healing rather than words of punishment for the period after the nation's most bitter struggle.

Since the time of the Civil War, other separations have marked America's history. Not long ago another American leader spoke both to and for the nation when he dreamed aloud of a healing between the races. As Lincoln dreamed of a reconciliation of America's regions, Martin Luther King dreamed of an America that would reconcile its races and put aside racial animosity and discrimination forever.

The Lincoln Memorial stands as a monument to the greatest of American political figures, and those who have sought to heal the divisions of their time, including Dr. King, have frequently come to it for inspiration. The Lincoln Memorial is more than a remembrance of things past in America. It is more than a place of repose or even a place of resolution for America's political tensions. It is both a tribute to tensions that have been resolved and a reminder of the inevitable reappearance of those national tensions that inexorably take the form of political separation. The Lincoln Memorial is, more than anything else, a reminder that there can be healing only when the tension that comes from such separations is both acknowledged and painfully remedied.

Unfortunately, the way in which Lincoln is posed in the Memorial is misunderstood by many who view the statue. Reflecting the political tensions that Lincoln would have resolved so generously as well as the racial tensions that Dr. King and others would have resolved with equal generosity in their time, a great tension informs the statue of Lincoln. Even though seated, Lincoln reveals a worrisome anticipation, particularly in his hands.

It was no accident that the sculptor Daniel Chester French depicted Lincoln in a posture of tension. Lincoln's unrest symbolizes not only the great tension of his day but also the successive political tensions that his memorial would share with those who stand before it to condemn fundamental human injustices that may exist in any day. Lincoln knew, as did King and others, that the continued well-being of the American nation depends above all on the honest bringing of the nation's political tensions before the public. As Lincoln knew that the struggle between the North and South would be neither easy nor short, King knew that the struggle between those who would maintain racism and those who would stamp it out would be bitter and divisive. Both correctly prescribed for the difficulties of their times because both first prescribed a full and honest disclosure of the tensions that marked their times.

Today, our nation has declined because of a tension among its peoples that is more hidden than any we have yet faced. Recall not only Jefferson's comments with regard to the need for constitutional regeneration. Recall also Jefferson's notion that two natural parties exist in all political societies. If, as Jefferson believed, the conservativism and radicalism of any polity are inherent, any polity must recognize its natural parties and design its political order so as to embrace them. Recall, finally, that Jefferson also spoke of the "different constitutions of the human mind."[1] Jefferson knew, as we Americans should know after 200 years of learning about ourselves, that different people think in different ways about all manner of things.

The political importance of Jefferson's insight into the inherent differences among human minds is even more important today than it was 200 years ago. His admonitions concerning each generation's constitutional obligation and his views of political parties and their linkages to different constitutions of the mind are all of a piece. Were Jefferson here to see the distortions of our government that the present generation has fostered, he would encourage the next generation to restore the nation by addressing the differences among human minds.

The lessons of America's greatest intellectual figure, Jefferson, are in this way fully consistent with the lessons of America's greatest political figure, Lincoln. Not surprisingly, Lincoln's understanding of the regional separation between our peoples and the tension that that separation caused, along with his position within a political party he made into one of our two great parties, evidenced not just the substance but the manner of his thinking. Even beyond his position on the great regional divide, Lincoln was predisposed to the aggregation of the public as a whole and the engaging of those issues that brought about that aggregation. Similarly, Jefferson's way of thinking had contributed to the growth of a political party and, in his outrage over the Alien and Sedition acts, for example, the growth of democratic opposition itself in his time.

The political reasons for our nation's decline today are more hidden than the reasons for the divisions between regions and races that were and in some ways still are so evident. Only a borrowing from, and a building upon, the manner of Jefferson's and Lincoln's political understandings, along with an acceptance of the worth of political opposition that naturally come from a knowledge of their *form* of understandings, will overcome America's decline.

More than anything else, the decline in America's political fortune is a result of the inability of the American people to engage in the necessary processes of political opposition and public choice. To a far greater degree than we would have imagined, we have suffered from choosing no political vision at all. The lack of such a vision is directly traceable to a public domain that has not been able to present a Jeffersonian or Lincolnian opposition to the orthodox, consensus based, political perspective of the American people.

America's inability to choose among political options is in part a result of the recently accelerated imbalances between our private-to-public and our legal-to-political domains that have been discussed here. But that inability to choose is as well, in part, a result of the imbalances between individual and majoritarian forms of representation. It further reflects a cumulative imbalance of not only centrifugal over centripetal structures but also the dominance of a consensus-driven, contractual way of thinking about government over a way of thinking that emphasizes the need for political opposition and political choice.

Were he alive today, Jefferson would recognize that the imbalance among the minds that dominate our government, the almost wholesale absence of that oppositional frame of mind that is more than anything else the core of democracy, has accentuated the consensually contractual, as opposed to the politically majoritarian, form of facing America's public difficulties. That imbalance has also accentuated the steady weakening of our political parties, as well as those parties' ability to engage in the creation of worthy public alternatives to current public policies. Both Jefferson and Lincoln would have decried the modern absence of strong political parties and of those public alternatives that parties best present to a polity in order to overcome history's divisions. They both would have decried these absences, even though Jefferson in his time in history found it necessary to create opposition and Lincoln in his time found it necessary to reconcile opposition.

The Next Generation

Only a commitment on the part of the next generation to revitalize our government and pointedly to rebalance the ways that America's institutions define, sharpen, and present alternative positions concerning the difficulties that the government faces will, in the long run, help our nation to overcome those difficulties. Let us not forget that the standard of democracy for which the antifederalists fought was raised in response to the federalists' argument that America's citizens be permitted something far less than full access to their government. That standard of democracy, now if not then, surely embraces the inclusion of peoples of all races, regions, colors, and national origins. But it also embraces a rebalancing of America's public institutions and a rebalancing of those preconstitutional political forces that undergird balanced political institutions.

Homage to Jefferson's admonition that each generation must revitalize its governmental institutions and homage to Lincoln's admonitions to acknowledge and heal the most severe of our nation's divisions is best paid by remembering those great figures' wisdom and foresight in the present political context. We serve the memory of Jefferson and Lincoln best, and we serve the cause of democracy best both in the United States and in the world, by revitalizing our democracy and revitalizing our understandings of how America's political institutions must act to properly be called democratic. The standard of democracy has always ascended and, if anything, become more difficult for each generation. But democracy will not wait for any nation that will not reach out to each new generation's standards for it. Jefferson and Lincoln would have us fulfill those new standards were they here today.

Note

1. Daniel J. Boorstin, *The Lost World of Thomas Jefferson*. Chicago, IL: University of Chicago Press, 1981, p. 172.

Index

Accountability, campaign
  consultants and, 58
Ancillary institutions,
    governmental
  Beltway consultants, 29, 37–41
  Congress and, 92–93
  singular vs. majoritarian interests
      and, 37–41
  elections industry and, 53
  as buffer between candidates and
      public, 58–60
  Congress and, 93
  incumbency and, 60–63
  former congressional members
      employed by, 99
  lawyer-lobbyists, 47–51, 76
  Congress and, 49–51, 92–93
  extension of national government
      to, 51
  the president and, 105–6
  public vs. private domain and,
      154–55
  Washington, D.C., living
      conditions and, 95–97
Anti-federalists, xiv, 39, 44
  Bill of Rights and, 34, 154
  Congress and, 90–91
  electoral process and, 57
  legal vs. political jurisdictions and,
      44

Anti-federalists *(continued)*
  public vs. private domain and, 5–6,
      26
Aristotle
  aristocracy and, 75
  political identification and, 65, 70,
      71, 73, 74

Baker v. *Carr,* 49, 151
Barron v. *Baltimore,* 67
Beltway consultants, 29, 37–
    41
  Congress and, 92–93
  singular vs. majoritarian interests
      and, 37–41
Bickel, Alexander, 45
Bill of Rights
  British, 40–41
  centrifugal vs. centripetal
      governmental arrangement
      and, 38
  First Amendment, 35
  public vs. private domain and, 6,
      10, 34–47, 154
  purpose of, 35
Brandeis, Louis D., 45
British Bill of Rights, 40–41
Brown v. *Board of Education,*
    48–49, 150, 151
Burke, Edmund, 92, 94

Campaign consultants
accountability and, 58
national vs. local interest and, 59
Campaigns, political
congressional, 109–10, 143
discussion of issues during, 57
financing of
congressional, 109–10, 143
political action committees and,
61–62
presidential, 110–12
Centrifugal vs. centripetal
governmental arrangement,
6–7. See also Ancillary
institutions, governmental
Beltway consultants and, 37–38
Bill of Rights and, 38
lawyer-lobbyists and, 48
Checks and balances, U.S.
government and, 84–85
Cities. See also Urban crisis
boundaries of, 150–52
role of, in governmental reform,
148–52
Virginian, 151
Civil War
Lincoln and, 155–56
the South and, 81
state sovereignty and, 66, 67, 74
Coke, Edward, 32, 36
Common law, 16, 31–33, 36
Congress, U.S., 89–101
ancillary institutions and, 92–93
post-congressional employment,
99
salary issue, 95–97
campaign financing and, 143
presidential influence on, 109–10
committees of, 90, 91
Connecticut Compromise and, 89–90
cost of congressional service and,
98–99
courts and, 46
fragmentation of, 90, 91

Congress, U.S. (continued)
lawyer-lobbyists and, 49–50
length of term and, 146–47
political parties and, 109–10
policy conventions and, 143–46
public vs. private domain and,
92–94, 99–100
relationship of, to government and
people, 93
representation in, 89–91
salary issue and, 94–98
ancillary institutions and, 95–97
staff members of, 91
structural imbalances in, 90–94
Connecticut Compromise, 89–90
Constitution, U.S. See also
Anti-federalists;
Preconstitutional order
balance of power in, 56–57
Bill of Rights
centrifugal vs. centripetal
governmental arrangement
and, 38
First Amendment, 35
public vs. private domain and, 6,
10, 34–47, 154
purpose of, 35
checks and balances in, 84–85
electoral process and, 56–57
English government and, 5–6
First Amendment, 35
legal vs. political jurisdictions and, 33
political parties and, 78
revitalization of, 3, 4, 13, 157–60
Seventeenth Amendment, 55
unwritten, xiii, 8, 12
Beltway consultants and, 37–41
Constitutional convention, proposed,
142
Consumption, 21
Corporations, private
American workers and, 23
corporate management and, 16–18,
25–26

Corporations, private *(continued)*
the environment and, 18–19
political legitimacy of, 17–18
productivity and competitiveness
of, 17–19, 22–24, 26–27
public vs. private domain and,
16–18
structure of, 17
world standards for, 23

Debt, national, 24
Decline, U.S., 3–5
causes of, 4–5
economic productivity and, 7–8
Democracy
electoral process and, 57–58
English, 33
global promotion of, 119–20
Democratic party, 76–77, 79–83,
86–88
governmental reform and, 86–87,
142
line-item veto and, 86
public vs. private domain and,
76–77, 80–81, 87
Republican restructuring of
government and, 80–83
role of, 87
the South and, 81–82
Distributional allocations, 20–22
Double-wage household, 8
Dred Scott ruling, 44

Economy, U.S.
distributional allocations and,
20–22
productivity and competitiveness
of, 22–24
decline of, 7–8, 17–19
government's role in, 21–22
Elections (electoral process), 9,
53–64
campaign consultants and, 58, 59
campaign financing and, 54–55

Elections *(continued)*
political action committees and,
60–63
costs of campaigns and, 53–54
elections industry and, 53
as buffer between candidates and
public, 58–60
Congress and, 93
incumbency and, 60–63
presidential, 55, 104–5, 110–12
representative democracy and,
57–58
Electoral College, 55, 104, 105
England
Bill of Rights in, 40–41
common law in, 16, 31–33, 36
Constitution and, 5–6
parliamentary law in, 32–33
Environment, 18–19
Europe, global age and, 121
European parliamentary system, U.S.
government compared to, 105,
108–9, 112

Federalists, 5–6
congressional representation and,
90–91
legal vs. political jurisdictions and,
44
Federal states, 65, 66
First Amendment, 35
Foundations, universities and,
136–38
Freedom of religion, 35
French, Daniel Chester, 156

global leadership, U.S., 115–22
international law and, 120
private institutions and, 116–22
decentralization of U.S.
government and, 121–22
Third World and, 118–19
promotion of democracy and,
119–20

Government, U.S. *See also*
Congress, U.S.; President; *and*
specific topics
ancillary institutions and, 154–55
former congressional members
employed by, 99
the president and, 105–6
restoration of preconstitutional
balances and, 63–64
Washington, D.C., living
conditions and, 95–97
balance of power in, 48
Beltway consultants and, 39–40
economic policy and, 21–24
European parliamentary system
compared to, 105, 108–9, 112
federal nature of, 66
legislative branch, 49
national economic policy and, 21
preconstitutional balances and, 5–8
the press and, 123–29
contractual nature of relationship,
125–26
divisions within government and,
124–25
ethical obligations and, 126–27
government's recent failures and,
127–29
maintaining access, 124–25
separation of powers in, 5
structural reform of, 139–52
cities' role in, 148–52
constitutional convention and, 142
local reforms and, 147–52
party policy conventions and,
142–46
the public and, 140–41
structure of, 80–87
checks and balances, 84–85
current gridlock, 85–87
Great Depression, 45

Hamilton, Alexander, 44, 45
Holmes, Oliver Wendell, 45

House of Representatives, 90
election of members to, 55
Hughes, Charles Evans, 44

International law, 120

Jackson, Andrew, 87
Jefferson, Thomas, 138, 155
on constitutional regeneration, 3, 4,
13, 157–60
on political parties, 79, 84, 86, 87,
157, 158

Kennedy, Edward M., 86
King, Martin Luther, 156, 157

Law, international, 120
Lawyer-lobbyists, 47–51, 76
Congress and, 49–51, 92–93
extension of national government
to, 51
Legal vs. political jurisdictions,
separation of, 31–41, 43–51, 56
Bill of Rights and, 34–37
English law and, 31–33, 36
Supreme Court and, 44–46, 48–49
Legislation, Supreme Court and,
44–46
Lincoln, Abraham
acknowledgment and reconciliation
of differences by, 155–60
as depicted in Lincoln Memorial,
156–57
Line-item veto, 85, 86
Lippmann, Walter, 123, 125–27
Local government. *See also* Urban crisis
structural reform and, 147–52
Lochner v. *New York,* 45
Locke, John, 32, 33, 36

Madison, James, 11, 12, 55, 56,
77–79
Marbury v. *Madison,* 44
Marshall, John, 44, 66–67

Middle class, 18
  decline of, 8

National debt, 24
National vs. local interest, 59
New York City, 68, 69

Officeholders, current, 8–10. *See
    also* Congress, U.S.; President;
    Elections
  alterations in constitutional order
      and, 8–10
  incumbency and, 8, 9, 60–63
  national vs. local interest and, 59
  political parties and, 8–9
  private interests of, 8–9, 22, 25
  public's relationship to, 8–9, 55–56
    elections industry and, 58–60
    incumbency and, 60–63
Parliamentary law, 32–33
Political action committees (PACs),
    61–62
Political consultants. *See* Beltway
    consultants; Campaign
    consultants
Political identification, 65
  cities and, 67–68, 70–74
Political vs. legal jurisdictions,
    separation of. *See* Legal vs.
    political jurisdictions,
    separation of
Political parties, 75–88. *See also*
    Democratic party; Republican
    party
  Congress and, 109–10
  Constitution and, 78
  isolation of officeholders from, 8–9
  Jefferson on, 79, 84, 86, 87, 157, 158
  policy conventions and, 142–46
  presidential campaigns and, 111–12
  public vs. private domain and,
      77–78
  relationship to government, 75–76
  role of, 75–78

Preconstitutional order, 5–7
  centrifugal vs. centripetal
      governmental arrangement
      and, 6–7
  legal vs. political jurisdictions and,
      31, 56
  public vs. private domain and, 5–6,
      15
  rebalancing of, 12
  restoration of, 63–64
  singular vs. majoritarian interests,
      56
President, 103–13
  ancillary institutions and, 105–6
  congressional campaign financing
      and, 109–10
  election of, 55, 104–5
    campaign, 110–12
  European parliamentary system
      and, 105, 108–9, 112
  line-item veto and, 85, 86
  mediocrity of, 103
  method of governance of, 106–7, 112
Press, national, 123–29
  conflict of interest and, 124, 127
  ethics of, 123–24
  government as source for, 123–29
    contractual nature of relationship,
        125–26
    divisions within government and,
        124–25
    ethical obligations and, 126–27
    government's recent failures and,
        127–29
    maintaining access, 124–25
  relationship to public, 123–28
    ethical obligations and, 126–27
Private institutions. *See also* Public
    vs. private domain
  global leadership and, 116–22
    decentralization of U.S.
        government and, 121–22
    Third World and, 118–19
    universities and, 134–38

Property rights, 46
Public, the
  officeholders' relationship to, 8–9,
    55–56
  elections industry and, 58–60
  incumbency and, 60–63
Public vs. private domain, 5–6,
    11–12, 15–29
  ancillary institutions and, 37–41,
    154–55
  banking and investment and, 23
  Beltway consultants and, 37–41
  Bill of Rights and, 6, 10, 34–47, 154
  Congress and, 92–94, 99–100
  corporations and, 16–18, 25–26
  Democratic party and, 76–77,
    80–81, 87
  distributional allocations and,
    20–22
  economic productivity and
    competitiveness and, 17–19,
    22–24, 26–27
  the environment and, 18–19
  legal changes in relationship
    between, 16
  national debt and, 24
  officeholders and, 22, 25
  political parties and, 77–78
  private legal community's
    influence and, 46–51
  Republican party and, 80
  states and, 66–67
  universities and, 133–38
  urban crisis and, 72–73
  Washington, D.C., living
    conditions and, 97

Reagan, Ronald, 80
Religion, freedom of, 35
Republican party, 79–80
  government gridlock and, 85
  line-item veto and, 85, 86
  public vs. private domain and, 80
  restructuring of government by, 80

Reynolds v. Sims, 151
Roosevelt, Franklin, 44–45, 87

Savings and investment, 21
School integration, 48
Senate, U.S., 90
Separation of powers, 5
Seventeenth Amendment, 55
Singular vs. majoritarian interests,
    56, 154–55
  Beltway consultants and, 37–41
  Bill of Rights and, 35–37
  Washington lawyer-lobbyists and,
    47–51
South, the, 81–82
States
  public vs. private domain and, 66–67
  sovereignty of, 66–67
  urban crisis and, 68–69, 72, 74,
    149–52
Suburbs, urban crisis and, 69, 72,
    150, 151
Supreme Court, U.S., 44–46, 48–49
  judicial excesses of, 48–49
  legislation and, 44–46
  urban crisis and, 69, 150–51

Taney, Roger, 44
Tax laws, economic productivity
    and, 21
Third World, 118–19
Tocqueville, Alexis de
    (Tocquevilleian form of
    government), 38, 39, 77, 103
Totalitarian political systems, 75

Unitary states, 65–66
United States. See also Government, U.S.
  foreign interests in, 117
  global leadership of, 115–22
    decentralization of U.S.
      government and, 121–22
    international law and, 120
    private institutions and, 116–22

United States *(continued)*
  promotion of democracy and,
    119–20
  Third World and, 118–19
University, 131–38
  importance of, 131–32
  private, 132, 134
  public, 132–38
    administration of, 133–34
    charge of, 132
    funding of, 134–38
    liberal arts in, 135
    openness about decision-making
      process and, 135–36
    private interests and, 133–38
  role of, 132
Urban crisis, 67–74
  causes of, 67–69, 72–73
  city boundaries and, 150–52
  national urban conventions to
    address, 149–52
  public vs. private domain and, 72–73

Urban crisis *(continued)*
  result of, 69–71
  solutions to, 73–74
  states and, 68–69, 72, 74, 149–52
  suburbs and, 69, 72, 150, 151
  Supreme Court and, 69, 150–51

Veto
  line-item, 85, 86
  presidential, 57
Virginia, cities in, 151

Warren, Earl, 45, 49, 150
Washington, George, 55–56, 116
Washington Beltway, 29–30. *See
    also* Beltway consultants
Washington, D.C., living conditions
    in, 95–97
Washington lawyer-lobbyists. *See*
    Lawyer-lobbyists
Wilson, Woodrow, 87
Workers, American, 23, 26

About the Author

William P. Kreml teaches political science at the University of South Carolina. He earned his Juris Doctor from the Northwestern University Law School and his Ph.D. from Indiana University. Kreml was a candidate for the Democratic senatorial nomination in South Carolina in 1980 and entered selected Democratic presidential primaries in 1984. Both campaigns dealt with the structural inadequacies of the American political system.